Film directors and other creative professionals must constantly re-invent ourselves, fight the blues, the self-doubt . . .We are increasingly forced to function as our own self-promoters and salespersons. It's not an easy to play both the Creative and the Business roles! This book not only provides insight into these challenges, but also gives us some real tools to get past them and make your career dreams come true.
- RANDA HAINES, Director of Oscar-nominated film, "Children of a Lesser God"

Jim Jermanok has written an extraordinarily wide ranging & deep self-help kit for today's entertainment business, drawing on his own wealth of experience in this treacherous field. Somehow, he manages to keep all this information clear, concise and often fun. Bravo!
- HARRY GREGSON-WILLIAMS, Award-winning Film Composer
("The Martian" "The Chronicles of Narnia" "The Shrek Series" "Passionada")

Finally someone who knows what they're talking about. Jim is the real deal!
- LENNY CLARKE, Actor, Comedian ("Rescue Me", "Sirens")

I would arm anyone setting forth with the hard-earned, perceptive insights that underlie this guide by Jim Jermanok to the hidden worlds where talent comes face to face with its first audience. Based on a lifetime spent creating the space to create art, Jermanok's book may prove to be a bible to anyone with a vision of what they wish to achieve but now wishes to be equipped with an understanding of the slow learning curve involved in finally discovering that one day you have become an overnight success.
- DERMOT BOLGER, Famed Irish Novelist, Playwright and Poet

As artists we all go through the creative pain/pleasure process. But that doesn't mean we have to suffer to survive. Suffering is a choice we can make or not make. Jim's book is not a complete pain killer, but a giant leap to end the unnecessary suffering.
- MEGUMI SASAKI, Award-winning Filmmaker ("Herb and Dorothy")

Creative career success is becoming harder than ever. Jim provides insights and practical skills that will give you a competitive edge to achieve your goals. It is invaluable!
- GEORGE T. NIERENBERG,
Acclaimed Documentarian ("Say, Amen Somebody" "No Maps on My Taps")

This is a no-nonsense roadmap for those who want to present their creative ideas with conviction and intelligence. I learned more reading this book for an hour than I have from all other such publications combined.

-BRYAN MILLER, former NY Times Restaurant Critic and Journalist, Author of bestselling Cooking for Dummies

BEYOND THE CRAFT: What You need To Know To Make A Living Creatively! is a must read for anyone who traverses down the treacherous path of pursuing a career in the arts, entertainment or media. Jermanok's succinct writing style mixed with a healthy dose of self-deprecating humor has led to an excellent book that all creative professionals and students will find useful in obtaining their career goals without having to solely rely on the typical gatekeepers: agents, managers and producers.

-YALE STROM, famed Klezmer musician, Author and documentarian ("The Last Klezmer")

Born from his own hard work and years of experience, Jim's book is a worthwhile personal and useful guide to any "creative" seeking or maintaining a career in the entertainment business. With firsthand knowledge, Jim addresses the truisms with practical advice and an insider's anecdotes.

-WENDY SAX, Producer ("Particle Fever", "Songcatcher")

Jim Jermanok understands the creative life as few others do. He has worked and taught at the highest level and helped many others achieve real results in this most competitive of industries. If you want to work as a creative this book will really help you.

- RAY YEATES, Actor, Director and Dublin City Arts Officer

*For **Beverly** and **Julius** who are with me always.*

BEYOND THE CRAFT:
What You Need to Know to Make A Living Creatively!

by

Jim Jermanok

Jim Jermanok
BEYOND THE CRAFT:
What You Need to Know to MakeA Living Creatively!

Publisher: Command Perfomance Publishing
Cover Design: Rosen Dukov
2016 ©All Rights Reserved

ISBN: 978-0-692-77576-9

TABLE OF CONTENTS

INTRODUCTION

I never thought I would write a motivational or self-help book in my life. Sure, maybe another screenplay, play, or teleplay. Or that great American novel or book of short stories, but a how-to book? Not my thing, style or goal.

For the past decade, I have spoken to hundreds of audiences worldwide at colleges and universities, film festivals, theaters and arts organizations, and acting and writing groups. Many of the questions from these audiences of aspiring, working and successful creative professionals were remarkably similar. Their occupations, goals or nationalities had little bearing. **Once I graduate or when I have a lull in my career, what do I do? What do I do in my career to be proactive to get to the next level? How do I stop relying on people —whether they are agents, managers or various gatekeepers: producers, casting directors, etc.—to succeed in my creative career? How do I make things happen?**

I searched in bookstores and on the web for books that cover the business side of the craft or simply creative career success. Nothing. Absolutely nada. I couldn't believe it. There are literally thousands of books about various crafts: acting, writing, screenwriting, directing, art, music—you name it, but nothing about creative career success. Yet, I knew from my speeches and workshops that there was a gigantic demand for this type of a book. A demand that wasn't being accommodated.

I also wanted to save creative professionals years. That's right, years. Not to mention, pain. When you are talented and not doing enough creatively, it really hurts. Many creatives are simply stuck and their careers and lives suffer as a result. I want to liberate them from their "creative career prisons" and inspire them to try other strategies to accomplish or succeed. By remaining stuck or inactive, many moons can indeed go by. But if you go for it, things will happen!

I also want to incorporate my own rather unique perspective or vantage point. There are no career advisory books by anyone who has worked at a large agency like ICM or CAA. Most agents at major agencies reap the benefits of working as agents or managers for their entire lives and eventually retire. A very tiny number are foolish enough to do what I did and quit a six-figure job to start at square one as a creative professional. That is, a person making a good living on the business side jumping to the risky and unpredictable creative side. I couldn't help it — I am creative and started getting jealous of my clients. What could I do? I wanted to be creative, damnit! I wanted to be part of the creative equation and not simply represent creative professionals.

So I began a long and continuing journey of almost two decades as an active writer, director and producer (and occasional actor) in film, TV, theater, and new media. Being on the front lines on the war of creative career success, if you will, as a present creative professional gives me a distinct advantage over those authors, so-called experts and university professors who may have given up long ago—if indeed they ever tried. My perspective is tried and true, extremely current and I'm still making things happen!

Both the agenting and filmmaking stages of my career have also allowed me to feed a thirst for knowledge I've had about creative career success for my entire life. How do creative people or artists succeed? What exactly separates them from the thousands or hundreds of thousands of other creative folks? Is it talent alone or are there other factors at play? What are those other factors? I have always been obsessed with the getting "the real scoop" about how celebrities and top-tier successful creative professionals actually succeed. I didn't want to hear the slick PR and/or sugarcoated versions that present themselves in magazine and newspaper articles or on talk shows. I wanted to know the unadulterated truth!

From the beginning of my tenure as an entertainment agent at ICM or International Creative Management, I asked a lot of questions from the names or celebrity clients themselves. Not only those I represented, but also those represented by my fellow agents. As a filmmaker, it was the same story. I asked all my successful friends, peers and colleagues how they did it—yearning for "the real scoop" yet again. I heard a lot of the same commonalities or descriptions over and over again. Those **habits, qualities, tools and practices**—that the names and the world's most successful actors, directors, writers, producers, artists musicians, singers, comedians, authors, journalists, photographers, designers and even business entrepreneurs—share. What they have in common in contrast to the majority of creative folks who fail to make a living in their chosen creative field. This, indeed, is the primary inspiration for this book.

After three decades of analysis of creative career success, I developed and created my own **unique philosophy, strategy and even vocabulary** to clearly convey these commonalities. I deliberately wrote specific, bite-sized and self-contained chapters in this book so you, my readers, can grasp, retain and use what you can to improve your careers and, in the process, perhaps, your lives. For me, there is no greater goal.

I also want to do my humble part in enabling the best and most talented to succeed, not necessarily the most connected or wealthiest (although I have nothing against either of these groups). It is my objective to empower those outside of the loop or clique, those who may not live in LA, NY or London, to achieve their creative goals and dreams. To get their work seen. No matter how gifted you may be, sometimes you may need a boost of knowledge and inspiration to attain that elusive next level of success. I dedicate this book to you!

* * *

THOSE EARLY YEARS: HOW I GOT MY START

On an early spring day in the 80s, I suddenly decided that I had enough of my freelance existence. I had been working in theater, commercials, music videos and feature films in a variety of capacities: assistant stage manager, sound technician, performer, assistant producer, associate producer, production assistant, production manager, grip and even gaffer (set electrician). Gaffer was a big mistake as I didn't know what I was doing and almost fried myself. I guess there is a limit to bullshitting your way into jobs.

Other Jobs. This was preceded by a slew of crazy and challenging survival jobs, from waiter to railroad construction worker to lifeguard. For a long period, I was the world's worst waiter, but I seemed to have a talent for scoring waiting jobs. Somehow, I obtained a prestigious waiting job at the Edwardian Room in the Plaza Hotel in NY. This was an ultra fancy schmancy space that was always packed. All of my "peers" were lifers and union members. I was partnered with another newcomer, Chris, who had come from a horse-and-carriage job guiding tourists in and out of Central Park. He had somehow killed his horse and needed to change his career.

From early on, my new "partner" Chris discovered my relative lack of experience and tried to sabotage me. He began complaining to the suave and smarmy maitre d', Luca, who had a near perfect track of pursuing and bedding single female hotel guests who were dining there alone.

Luca ignored my so-called partner for quite some time until the accident. I was holding a giant silver tray containing three full plates of chateaubriand steaks way above my head. From the kitchen to the dining floor, the waiter's mandatory journey resembled the Bataan

Death March. One had to avoid numerous kitchen bee workers, hot ovens, abusive morons, other waiters and multiple obstacles along the way—not to mention navigating different floor levels, stairways, long corridors and a very, very slippery floor that I somehow managed to cross a hundred times before.

Not this time. I literally somersaulted like a cartoon character. The plates went a flying and important dinner guests complained about the delay of their Chateaubriands. Of course, when my partner found out, a fiendish smile covered his face. He immediately complained to Luca. By the end of my shift that evening, I was toast.

Another waiting job had fallen through and I was persuaded to go to an employment office and see which other jobs were available. Slim pickings but there was a railroad construction "opportunity" that was looking for someone urgently. You think stage fright is hard? No, this was the most ridiculously demanding job I've ever had.

A few basics about railroad construction work. If it's ninety degrees outside, it's 110 degrees at the railroad because of the conduction of the metal tracks. At this time, a black gooey and carcinogenic substance called Creosote covered all the wooden ties. This stuff required a really long bath and continuous scrubbing to have a prayer of removing it from one's body. Not a particularly fun task because after each shift, because by this time, I was exhausted to the point of collapse. All of my fellow workers—essentially he-men and macho male monsters—seemed to relish the work with the gusto of worshippers at a Biblical retreat. In contrast, I hated every single minute.

Things did not improve when my work crew found out I was a recent college graduate. Their constant ribbing and teasing was further elevated when they decided my productivity was not at par with theirs. Taunts like "You should know how to do it better, college boy!" or "Need a degree for that jack hammer?" continued unabated until something miraculous happened: an overly tan, quiet, young Clint Eastwood type began defending me for some reason. "He's doing the best he can," Nick declared. "Leave him the fuck alone." The teasing slowed down, but it had been seven weeks of hell and I was finished. This was my proverbial straw in the camel's back. Perhaps, I should've stuck it out for a few more months, but it's important to know when it's time to leave--and that's exactly what I did.

My lifeguard job was much, much easier. It was on the roof pool of a swanky Upper East Side condo building. I really got along with my stern, disciplined Norwegian boss with whom I had bonded like thieves by talking about Norway as much as I possibly could. I realized what was required and went for it. "What was the longest distance you skied cross-country or Nordic style?" "What was Oslo like in the 40s?" "How do you survive in the Midnight Sun?" Norway maintained a serious resistance against the Nazis in World War II— our frequent conversations on this topic definitely cemented our friendship. No American he had ever encountered knew anything about Norway. I did the requisite research and tried my damndest to stay on topic.

For days on end, I would hang out on the pool deck and mingle with the scattering of well-heeled guests who made their way there. Otherwise, I would play with my navel, ponder my existence, and procrastinate over my then unattainable creative career options. And I read the news ferociously. Usually all three NY papers: *The Daily News, The NY Post* and *The NY Times*. In those days, the *Times* was very thick, but I managed to read it cover to cover and even tried halfheartedly to finish the crossword puzzle. I studied all the profiles about successful creative professionals: actors, performers, directors, writers, and producers that seemed a million miles away. Rarely did I read about how they actually made it and this became a lifelong source of curiosity. I guess I could've been much more productive, but I was clearly drowning in avoidance. Creative career avoidance.

The lifeguard gig was a very hard job to quit, but I had run out of Norwegian topics--and started getting jealous of those *Times* interviewees. One of the building's residents was a divorcee who was always sipping martinis out of a Tupperware container. I guess she made out well. She got me a gig on a movie set and I began the described variety of theater and film jobs for the next few years.

The last job got me thinking. I was PA'ing on a movie about gangs and boxers. It was weeks of night shoots in a very dangerous and rather desolate Brooklyn neighborhood that has since been developed and gentrified. But then it was seriously dangerous. I was all alone and protecting tens or maybe, hundreds of thousands of dollars of movie equipment from actual, real-life gang members, scary criminals and other psychos. The ones who could only speak English with a pronounced Brooklyn accent. There never seemed to be any fellow crewmembers in sight. All of these creeps could have whacked me and probably gotten away with it. While you digest the irony, I just want you to know that I was stressed out of my mind. Really petrified. But I stood it out because my then live-in girlfriend and I needed the money.

We had plans to marry later in the year and this last piece of work helped convince me to try to obtain a 9 to 5 job with a steady paycheck. But I wasn't sure which job or direction to pursue. I was a kid in a candy store and was simply overwhelmed by all the choices. Should I pursue a production company, commercial production company, theater or theater company, TV network, TV cable network, advertising agency, literary agency or entertainment agency? Or should I try to be an assistant or right-hand man to a successful actor, director, writer or producer. Absolutely no clue or leaning.

In a moment of clarity or perhaps, indecision, I decided to go for all the possibilities at once and see what happens. This was not a designed or numbered approach that a canny salesperson would pursue, but I just couldn't decide. Making choices in timely and effective manner is something I still struggle with today. But now I realize that it's not so important. That making a choice is better than not making one. It's that simple. Just make the Goddamned choice. You can always go back. Most of the time, anyway.

In the pre-Web era, it's difficult to convey how hard it was to find all the addresses of these entertainment companies. Sure, the big ones were a snap, but the smaller companies and creative individuals were often next to impossible to access. A complete directory of these entertainment offices did not exist at the time. But I had visited the Library of Performing Arts in the Upper West Side of Manhattan a few times and happened to know that it had a number of various show business directories in its reference area. These were rather very specific if not esoteric. They were also quite expensive and difficult to own.

One enterprising and optimistic day, there I was at the library with a bag of dimes copying these directories like a man on a mission. There was at least eight or nine of them. I stapled them and now they were mine. Then I starred those entertainment companies that looked appealing. For some quirky reason, I decided to spread them out on the large table and create my own Manhattan address grid on separate lined pad. Each page had a street heading like 58th Street or 59th Street. I still have no idea how I managed to do this. I am not particularly organized. No one ever advised me about this job searching technique. But I innately knew I had to do something distinctive to succeed in the creative world. So I completely made up this strategy or system.

I decided to first focus on Midtown since many of these entertainment companies were located there. Starting on the east side or First Avenue, I would begin on East 59th Street and jot down all those addresses of entertainment targets until 11th Avenue or the western reaches of West 59th Street. The addresses were carefully written in geographical order. Then I planned to snake around to West

58th Street and make my way, avenue by avenue to East 58th Street and First Avenue. Then I would go to East 57th Street and on and on.

In the course of the next day or two, I had completed writing this address grid until I got to 37th Street. I figured I would go on to another neighborhood like Greenwich Village when I had Midtown finished. It was time to begin.

Without a day's rest, I grabbed a used briefcase, which became host to a giant pile of my resumes. I soon found myself at East 59th Street and First Avenue. I was on my way. In these pre- 9-11 days, you could walk in almost anywhere. Okay, sometimes I had to bullshit the receptionist or doorman, but you could get to almost anyone in this manner.

I was suddenly scrambling in more production companies, commercial production companies, theaters, network cable network offices, advertising agencies, chic high-rises and entertainment agencies than I ever knew existed. I met hundreds of successful or apparently successful actors, directors, writers or producers. I handed out my resumes to as many people as I could and somehow scribbled their names—when they would give me their names, that is. With writing that normally resembles chicken scratch, many of these names would later be illegible. No matter, I kept at it the next day and the next. Again, I was a man on a mission.

I would hand my resume to multiple people at the same office, and at companies/offices that weren't on my initial list. In short, anyone who would take one. I said I was "looking for an opportunity" and tailored my approach as much as I could to the specific business at hand. One business that wasn't on the list was a camera rental place, where I told them that "I love lenses" or some such nonsense. Most people were impressed by my spunk or chutzpah (nerve). Others were fascinated by my approach and asked me multiple questions. Still other potential employers took the time to generously give me career advice. And boy, did I ever need it.

There were some protective or obnoxious jerks who refused to take my resume or gave me a dressing down. Others harassed, teased or patronized me, but I didn't let them bother me. Even then, I had a feeling that rejection or coping with rejection was part of the game. I kept on moving. Isn't that what life's about? I had to finish Midtown, didn't I?

Within a few days, I found my way to West 51st St. and dusk. I stopped and went home to Astoria in nearby Queens. I was exhausted, but good news had arrived. I had enough interviews and opportunities to suspend the search. Within a week, I had six job offers: from a film distributor, producer, theater company and yes, that camera rental place. I guess they also liked lenses. But the final job offer clinched it, an opportunity to begin the "*training program*" at International Creative Management or ICM.

At the time, ICM was the largest entertainment, literary and newscasting agency in the world. The so-called ICM Training Program was not an easy program to get into. I found out after I got accepted that they received literally thousands of applications from lawyers, MBA's and other recipients of esteemed graduate degrees from elite institutions of higher learning. I was very fortunate. In addition, nepotism was alive and well and I would learn later that many of the trainees had parents in the industry or knew someone inside the company.

I soon discovered that the "training" was solely *on-the-job* training like much of entertainment world. There were never any seminars or classes. There was never an opportunity to ask questions of the agents, most of whom frowned upon any unnecessary contact with the trainees. But the other trainees and I had many discussions and we all learned from each other through a variety of means including: eavesdropping, filling in for assistants, delivering mail and packages, messangering (doing a "run") or performing other errands for the agents and/or their star clients.

Each of us was assigned to our own beat, a department or floor that we were responsible for distributing inter-office and external mail. With my Ivy League (Cornell) degree and pride safely in pocket, I found myself having to answer to the insufferable demands of assistants. Don't get me wrong. Some were kind, entertaining and informative. But the others were demanding, bitchy and condescending in a number of inventive ways. Again, many of them were assistants purely because they or their family knew someone in the company—allowing them to bypass the bottom or mailroom rung. However they behaved, I attempted to accommodate them, but was not always successful. Some just didn't like the trainees and that was that.

The one sole opportunity for revenge was to read their mail. And to read the mail of everyone else. The best chance to do this was doing a one way or special delivery from one agent to another. We could go to the bathroom or some hidden staircase and study the communication. We checked out the contracts and how agents dealt with fellow agents and their clients. We studied how they kissed the asses of senior agents and executives. These documents, indeed, became our education.

Learning can be fun. A trade article at the time described the treatment of trainees and assistants as: "At ICM, they eat their young." ICM had rival and competing factions or fiefdoms. The top agents were essentially at odds with one another. This led to the lieutenants or agents in one camp warring with agents from other camps or factions, if you like. In other words, agents were often in conflict with one another. Their behavior and communication with each other proved to be very revealing. Stress was rampant and the gossip was nonstop. *The Art of War* was mandatory reading in a place like this.

On the other hand, many of the agents were wonderful people. They would take the time to give us lessons or answer questions if we dared to ask. They would often allow us to sit in their office as they spoke to clients, or other agents in NY, LA or London. We could also have a valuable glimpse into how they negotiated with buyers such as studio, television or publishing executives. We were able to get a glimmer of the sacred code of the agency business: deal making. Each agent had his or her own style. Some were gentle, quiet and classy. Others were as loud and obnoxious as the overbearing stereotype of an agent.

One of the former group was Milton Goldman. Milton was a classy gentleman in his late sixties who represented the likes of Laurence Olivier, Ralph Richardson, John Gielgud, Noel Coward, Alec Guinness, Douglas Fairbanks Jr., and Helen Hayes (who I repped for a few years upon his passing). Unlike many of my present generation who can be cutthroat and territorial, Milton would have frequent soirees or parties where he would invite everyone. He took pride in introducing people without an expectation of anything in return. Milton took a liking to me and would throw me film and theater premiere tickets now and then. I would also occasionally escort his primarily elderly female clients and friends to such events and I loved it because I was able to meet a wealth of dignitaries. Once I was literally a "walker" for Radie Harris, the legendary Broadway columnist at the "Night of 100 Stars" Broadway charity benefit and wouldn't you know, I met most of them.

From the minute I walked into ICM's West 57th Street office, I strived to meet, question and bond with the ICM clients. Most of the ICM clients were either household names or at least recognizable to the "civilian" or non-industry audience. At first, I was star-struck at the literally dozens upon dozens of names I encountered each week. From movie stars like Robin Williams, Meryl Streep and Ben Kingsley to recording legends like Ozzie Osbourne and James Taylor to writing legends like Thomas Wolfe and Arthur Miller. Oscar, Emmy,

Tony and Pulitzer Prize winners galore. I was fascinated by the royal treatment that the biggest superstars received from everyone—even the top agents.

The trainees were all reading the trades, *Variety* and *Hollywood Reporter* cover to cover in those days in an attempt to get a handle on the business. We liked to compare what we knew or discovered confidentially to what was presented in the trades. Sometimes they got it right, but usually there were discrepancies. The trades are prone to hyperbole or, at least, overly optimistic.

The mood of the office was definitely affected by the ups and downs of the careers of these clients. There was a giddiness that permeated throughout the office if a prospective star client was visiting or better yet, was signing on to become a new ICM client. When one of our clients won a major award or booked a new series or important film, everyone was psyched. When a major client left the agency or was fired from an important gig, there was an anxious pall that spread throughout the office. There was also an uneasy feeling if an agent was fired or fled to a rival. But this didn't happen all that often.

The personal encounters my new friends, the fellow trainees, and I had with the major agents or the steady stream of names became the daily lore of the place. Some encounters we laughed or fretted about for many months to come. As you could predict, many were happy with their lives, success or stardom. Other clients seemed oddly dissatisfied or downright miserable. Many were calm, cool and collected while their counterparts were continually anxious or on the verge of a breakdown.

Although this was a source of nonstop conversation and gossip among us, I was never that interested in their psychology or pathology for that matter. Instead, I was always on a quest to discover their secrets of achieving creative success. Not simply the manufactured or polished success stories that one reads in periodicals or sees on TV talks shows and interviews. No, I wanted to know how they *really* made it. The real scoop if you will.

Of course, I wanted to absorb this knowledge to apply to my slightly ambitious self—you know, the obvious reasons. But even early on, I understood that there was no formula to such success and committed myself to learning what qualities these clients possessed that led to their achievement.

I was also beginning to understand these qualities varied depending on the star. Some were insanely talented and their skills propelled them to the top. The "cream rises to the top" explanation which I expected. However, there were a sizable and surprising number of clients who had average or limited talents and yet, here they were enjoying extreme success with the super talented. This discovery motivated me to learn what I could about those qualities and commonalities these clients shared—whatever their relative professions.

Now and then, one of my fellow trainees would be fired for a relatively small transgression, at least it seemed that way to me, a loyal friend. They went AWOL for an extra hour on a messenger run, asking too much of a client or agent, forgetting to deliver something or worst of all, delivering a confidential note or memo to the wrong target. Another no-no was stealing swag in the form of CDs, book or videos--or actually being caught looking at someone's mail.

It could also be simply pissing off one of the big dictatorial bosses in a myriad of ways. These occasional job guillotines had the intended effect of keeping us in check, but since we were all guilty of many of these "crimes," one never knew if being summoned to the boss's office was for termination or advancement.

I had now worked more than six months as a mailroom trainee and I was dying for a promotion. I felt like I learned what I could and it was time to put it into practice. To sign and interact more with clients and to have stronger relationships with the buyers and agents. To make my own deals! When was I going to have the chance? I was summoned and found out there was another opening for Agent's Assistant. I had been to several of these interviews and thought I did a fine job, but usually lost out to those who were more connected than me.

Well, this interview was going to be mine. I researched and analyzed my prospective agent boss as much I could. I found out about his clients and by the time we met, I was ready. As a mailroom trainee, I was making less than 20G in NY. Try living in NY on that salary. My friends from Cornell were beginning to graduate with law school and MBA degrees which allowed them to choose among near six-figure salary offers. Here I was trying to deal on a measly twenty grand. Not to mention, marriage was waiting for me in a mere month.

The pressure was on. I walked into his office and did my best to understand what kind of person this agent was. Randy Chaplin was clearly a family man, who lived in the suburbs. A very, very nice guy with integrity. That's right, there are some agents who fit that bill. He was in a band and played a few instruments. I exuded confidence way beyond my experience. We got along great and realized that we had much in common. Most important, Randy's take on the agency business, ICM and even life were very similar to mine. He spoke of all the other candidates he was going to interview. I shook his hand and went back to delivering office mail with my Ivy League degree.

My mailroom boss called me in the next day to sign some papers, which is how I was informed that I obtained the Agent Assistant's job. My new agent boss was fantastic and I worked my ass off to complement his efforts. To make him look good. Isn't that the job description of any assistant? Soon, I gained his trust and was helping him select and sign clients as well as foster his bonds with those buyers who could hire such talent. He was open and generous about letting me hear his actual negotiations (via speakerphone or another extension) and study his sales technique, which I found to be a bit aggressive at first.

In the coming months I was actually making small deals by myself--which my boss would approve and sign. I was getting to know a wide range of ICM clients from actors to directors to authors and even newscasters. I was in a unique position to get to know them on the phone and in person at various events where they attended or performed. By servicing them really well—returning their phone calls rapidly, doing their travel and lodging arrangements when necessary, making connections for them, advising them about recent industry news and developments with particular relevance to them---and, of course, negotiating great fees, I gained their trust and even friendship.

Yes, Virginia, stars need friends too. They particularly enjoy having genuine people in their life who don't kiss their ass constantly or agree all the time—although there are exceptions who solely surround themselves with "yes men." A few of these former clients have stayed friends to this day.

With such familiarity and friendship I was now free to ask them all the questions I wanted. When I focused on how they made it, I was blown away by their answers Most came clean and gave me their true, unpolished and unadulterated accounts. However a few clamed up, lied or were generally defensive. It became abundantly clear that although talent certainly helped, it was, by no means, an absolute predictor of creative success. **Instead, several other magical common qualities essential for success began to stand out: distinguishing yourself from the pack, self-promotion, marketing oneself, and impressive networking efforts and abilities—to name a few.**

These qualities are the genesis for this book and much of the content of my workshops worldwide.

* * *

LATER LESSONS:
DISPATCHES FROM MY CAREER

To be at a place like ICM or Paramount Studios, CBS, HBO, CAA, MTV, Condé Nast or any of the major entertainment companies early in one's career can be a huge step above simply being a solo freelancer for the entirety of your career. If you have time to pay your dues in a place like this, I strongly suggest it. Not that you have to spend more than a few years at it--if that. But it is an exceptional training ground for how the business works—even though the training is usually not particularly structured or organized.

There are a number of lessons you will hopefully learn whatever your initial resistance. You will hopefully learn not to be intimidated by anyone, whatever their level of achievement. You will also learn not to envy anyone, even A-list stars, because everyone has their own journey and life burdens to bear. Most importantly, you will learn how to schmooze and network with acquaintances, colleagues and future friends all in the same dysfunctional business. You will learn what type of networking works and doesn't work for you. With the high numbers of people you will meet, you will figure out how to read people--an incredibly important skill in succeeding creatively. Are they worth collaborating or partnering with or better yet, befriending? Or do they simply justify keeping in touch with because you never know? You will need to continually sharpen your judgment in these areas.

Most importantly, if you join a entertainment monolith, you can't help but make a giant foundation of contacts that you will draw upon for your entire career. A strong network that will be the source of friendship, news, gossip and future employment.

Contact accumulation is the goal. Of course, quality of contacts is always more important than quantity of contacts. You always need to be very selective, but the simple truth is: **The larger the network you have, the more opportunities you will have.** If you don't cross paths with one of these media monoliths early in your career, you will be at a deficit compared to those who have done their time at one of these media factories.

Back to my ICM years. I was finally promoted from the mailroom to Assistant Agent. I now had a cubicle to call my own. I began to read contracts, help sign clients and speak to them regularly. Like one does in high school, I got to know almost everyone at the agency, assistants and agents at my office in NY as well as London and LA. I learned the essential skills of promoting a client's career: sales, marketing, pitching, publicity, negotiating. I also learned how to get along with a variety of personalities and egos.

Then it happened. After ten months at the job, I walked in one morning and found my boss's office completely vacant except for a lonely Rolodex. I immediately panicked and then slowly walked to my office. Were we both fired? It turned out that Randy had defected to our rival agency, William Morris, and I was offered his job by the President. I was off to the races (the complete story is in the **Fake It Til You Make It** Chapter).

For the next eight years, I would represent dozens of amazing clients like Alan Arkin, John Chancellor, E.L. Doctorow, Helen Hayes, Ben Kingsley, Shirley MacLaine, Arthur Miller, Dudley Moore, Henry Winkler and the one and only H. Norman Schwarzkopf. I was able to get to know most of them rather well and once again ask them questions about their lives and careers. The real unpolished scoop on how they really made it. Although many of their journeys differed in various ways, their habits, attitudes and certain traits were relatively similar. These habits, attitudes and traits form the chapters and foundation of this book.

Many other well-known clients came and went. It always hurt me when a client left, but often it was just a matter or them leaving ICM for another agency. Or their manager felt the need to intervene foolishly for some reason having little to do with our servicing.

The hottest client I helped to represent was not in show business at all—at least at the time. It was the legendary 4-star General H. Norman Schwarzkopf right after his enormous and instant fame as leader of the first Iraqi or Persian Gulf War aka Operation Desert Storm. He described the war in a strong, forthright manner on TV and soon, the whole world was at his feet. At the time in 1991, he was the first major military hero since MacArthur. A white-hot media sensation and media darling. He could do no wrong and everyone wanted a piece of him. When I say everyone, I mean everyone. World leaders, corporate CEO's, TV networks, publishing companies, associations, and universities—you name it.

As one of a number of agents that made the cut to meet with him (arranged by Marvin Josephson, one of the greatest agents in history and the Chairman and founder of ICM), I was summoned to Southern Command Center in Tampa where Schwarzkopf was the big boss.

It was a contrast for my staff and me to suddenly deal with the military. Every single detail was discussed in depth. We were told that I would be having lunch with the General on early Sunday afternoon, and believe you me, there was no room for negotiation. "You will meet the General in thirteen hundred hours. You will be there thirty minutes early at section B 7 in the southeast compound." That kind of craziness. A constant reminder that he was still a freaking FOUR STAR GENERAL! In a few days, I was to meet the biggest media superstar in many years.

I immediately began to read everything I could find on him. Mostly articles in newspapers and magazines. I was not about to allow myself any room for error as there was no second chance with this guy. At a small gift shop in JFK airport, I snapped up one of those quickie paperback biographies that appear out of nowhere when someone becomes a news sensation. For the next ten hours, I read that book slowly and thoroughly. For all intents and purposes, I essentially memorized it.

I arrived early Saturday evening and stayed in a modest hotel near the base. And reread the book. Seriously. I rented a car to basically drive the quarter mile to the base. Despite an abundance of manpower, they couldn't pick me up for some reason. So I drove my rented vehicle for literally a minute to the base.

I was picked up by a series of "Yes, sir, No sir" types who, predictably, were not very revealing. They also spoke about the General like he was the second coming, which had the effect of making me even more nervous than I was. I waited and waited and suddenly the General appeared. He was not disarming in the least, but I decided not to be intimidated. He did not delay in letting me know that "yesterday's lunch guest was the Queen of England." You know, as in Elizabeth Windsor. She apparently flew in with her private jet and thanked the General for his military success personally. Now, I was intimidated.

General H. Norman Schwarzkopf was clearly a man who liked others to listen to his every word. A man who did not like to argue or tolerate disobedience. I was on my best behavior as his obsequious personal chef presented us with a scrumptious chopped salad. Over the next two hours, I found a way to interject everything I knew about his life. "What was it like to move to Iran at the age of twelve?" was one bizarre question I found myself uttering. I also brought up his military dad and asked about his lead role in the investigation of the 1932 Lindbergh kidnapping. I also asked about his "three Silver Star Medals, two Purple Hearts and the Legion of Merit" he earned at Vietnam. He loved that question!

Highly intelligent but not overtly intellectual, the General also asked me several questions about the kind of fees he could expect, how much time was involved, and what I though of my competitors. I was dismissed and a week later found out that I was the one chosen to represent him. For the next few years I obtained record-breaking fees for Schwarzkopf to speak at various countries, corporations and associations. He received the highest fees ever offered to a speaker at the time. For the next six months, I literally had cabinet ministers and CEOs calling all the time. It was not an easy job to say no to these leaders, but I had no choice. The General did not want to accept more than two or three talks a month.

It was exhausting but lucrative work. I also was tasked with doing insanely detailed (think military again) itineraries for each appearance. For example, "After the Danish Prime Minister, you will be meeting the Danish Defense Minister at 1400 hours in the east courtyard of the castle. Then a meet-and-greet with the following other cabinet ministers, etc." I remember once he ruined a Thanksgiving Day family reunion by urgently asking for impossible to obtain itinerary details of a trip several months in the future. Despite such efforts and monetary rewards, General Schwarzkopf never once thanked me for my work. Never once gave me a gift or compliment. He started the last conversation we ever had with "Per the schedule for..." "Per???" I just made you a million dollars in the past month! He always treated me like a military minion, but I am truly grateful for the experience.

In contrast to the General, I loved working with many of my other clients. I'm proud to call myself a friend of multiple Academy Award-winning actor Alan Arkin. He is not only a superb, popular actor but a solid human being. From the moment we met, we had a connection. He is hilariously funny as you may expect, but is also a deep and spiritual man. He was written a number of interesting books about his spiritual journeys, creativity and life. I remember in the first year of representing him, he discovered that I was a classical music moron and he sent me several homemade cassettes featuring famed American composer Aaron Copeland. Alan also makes a mean waffle.

Another client, anchorman John Chancellor, also had a lasting effect on me. Despite being one of the most successful newsmen in history, John was always humble, wise and gentlemanly. He never took himself or his job too seriously. He was never too busy to have a meaningful conversation. John's take on the news stories, however complex, was clarifying and sensible. He had the ability to cut through the bullshit and get to the essence of each story. It was always a pleasure to converse with him and I miss the guy.

I had the honor of representing Helen Hayes for last few years of her life. It was admittedly not a very taxing position. She really did not want to work that much. In short, she was the epitome of class as her close friend Dame Astor would always attest. I loved to see them rib one another. Ms. Hayes would often invite me to various functions. One was a benefit for a favorite Catholic charity of the Kennedys. Upon arriving, I was met by Ted Kennedy, and his sisters Jean Kennedy Smith and Eunice Kennedy Shriver. I couldn't believe how they all introduced themselves to me. "Hello Jim, I'm Ted Kennedy." I felt like saying, "Let me get that last name again? K-Kenadee?" but restrained myself and simply smiled in astonishment. Like everyone else, they treated the First Lady of Theater like family.

One day, I got a call from Steven Spielberg's people and then from the great director himself. They wanted Helen Hayes to take the role of the 90-year-old Granny Wendy in "Hook," his upcoming film inspired by Peter Pan starring Robin Williams as an adult Peter Pan. I immediately called Ms. Hayes and FedExed the script to her in Nyack. She read it at once and passed. I told her it was Steve Spielberg. "Shouldn't you think about it?" "Oh, alright, I'll give it one more read." Two days later, Helen Hayes called me. "It simply is not up to par—for me." I told Spielberg that Helen Hayes had definitely passed. He couldn't believe it and when I told him she was going to be in LA, he asked to meet her. I organized a meeting between Ms. Hayes and Steven Spielberg and they had an amazing time together. But even Steven Spielberg was not able to convince Helen Hayes. She had impeccable standards and was not willing to compromise for anyone or any fee. The part eventually went to the wonderful actress Maggie Smith, a fellow ICM client—so the commission wasn't lost.

One day in 1993, I received a call from the BBC. They wanted to do a documentary about two legends: Nelson Mandela and my client Arthur Miller. Mandela had just been released a couple of years prior and was busy campaigning to be the first black leader of South Africa. He was a great admirer of Arthur Miller and his play "The Crucible" which had inspired Mandela during his 27 years of imprisonment. And both men were the same age: 75.

It seemed like a slam-dunk. I called Arthur Miller and he listened to what I had to say and then passed. It was a long trip and, despite his age, he was busy with numerous projects. I told him how historic this could be and how much Mandela admired him. Miller told me the feeling was mutual, but he just didn't have the time. I was a Rotary Exchange student to Johannesburg when I was 17 and was very well informed about South Africa's rather complex and changing political climate.

After a few more phone calls promoting the magic, beauty and fascination of one of my favorite countries (I've been to 80!), Arthur Miller finally agreed to go. I had a few meetings with Miller at his apartment in New York where I discussed South Africa's political history and complexities in detail. An intellectual workingman with insatiable curiosity, Miller thirsted for every detail and nuance. His constant appetite for learning was impressive. A couple of months later, Miller and his brilliant photographer wife, Inga Morath, left for South Africa. They had the time of their lives. A Mandela-Miller BBC documentary aired later that year.

As an ICM Agent, I was always meeting clients, names and newsmakers for breakfast, lunch, drinks, and dinner. It was thrilling but took a toll on my domestic life. I did not spend enough time at home with my wife and she never wanted to go to these affairs. For this and many other typical reasons that lead to a break-up, we eventually divorced. It was the low, low point for me. Someone advised me at the time "when love fails, follow your dreams." Being an agent for the rest of my life was not my dream; bring creative once again was.

I went to hundreds of film, theater and book premieres. Often I was the only person I never heard of at these parties. This has a daunting effect on you. I wondered why I never took more of an opportunity to become creative. Why I never gave it a shot. I gradually started craving to be creative again. At times, I even began to feel jealous of my clients.

One thing I knew, I had definitely conquered my job. I learned how to represent creative professionals well. How to negotiate on their behalf and propel them to the next plateau or earning level of their careers. Sure I could keep at it for years to come, but the challenge was fading fast and I was getting bored. Has the challenge in your present position dimmed? I loved most of my clients and they loved me. I always told them the truth and they respected that. But I started getting tired of the daily sales grind. If you take away the "glamour," that's what being an agent is: a glorified salesperson. I knew it was time to go. Despite a six-figure income and sizable expense account, I was ready to risk my future on becoming a creative professional, not representing a creative pro, but becoming one once again.

To the surprise and horror of many, I finally quit. Then I decided to step back from my career and take a break. So many people never do this in their lives. They believe their careers should span from college graduation to retirement. Not me. I needed to, if I may coin a phrase: "de-careerize." It was glorious to be liberated from my career track for a while. It allowed me to think, just think. Most people do not take the time to do this each day. Soon, I was able to clarify my goals and strategy. I also attempted to answer all those nagging and paranoid questions that were bubbling in my mind. What am I going to do? Should I obtain another salaried job? Business or creative or both? Am I good enough? Which medium should I dive into?

A few months later I wrote and produced a film, "Clear Cut," starring the gifted Calista Flockhart ("Ally McBeal") in one of her first film roles and the amazing actor, writer and "Renaissance Man" Stephen Fry. It drew praise and appeared at several film festivals.

When I returned to the US and attempted to resume my career, I scheduled a long trip to LA. I arranged to meet with many people including Just Betzer, the Danish Oscar winning producer behind "Babette's Feast" and many other quality films. I loved the film and started cutting out trade articles about him. One of the most important uses of the hyped industry trades is to discover those individuals that inspire you--with whom you could collaborate creatively with in an ideal world.

We got along swimmingly and Just pitched me an idea that I thought my brother and writing partner Stephen and I could handle. Just commissioned us to write it and we were off to the races. Betzer loved the script! "It will be made!" Unfortunately, it never was, but now we had experience working with a seasoned producer.

Several other scripts sold, but we became frustrated at not having them made. Unfortunately, this is a very common frustration among screenwriters, whether a neophyte or veteran. There is always some obstacle that rears its ugly head to block your script from becoming a film. They call it development hell for a reason. Instead of complaining with fellow writers which is awfully fun and tempting, I decided to aggressively meet as many producers and financiers as I possible could. I would try to push a couple of scripts we had available, but always be open to the dreams of potential partners as well.

1In the world of theater, I have been fortunate to have directed and produced over fifteen professional and regional productions ranging from *G.R. Point* to *Rosencrantz and Guildenstern are Dead*. One of my latest directorial efforts, *The Tramway End*, (the American premiere of esteemed Irish playwright-novelist Dermot Bolger) was presented for three months at the Chelsea Playhouse. It is about an Irish immigrant who lives in Germany and starred the renowned, talented Irish actor and director, Ray Yeates, who is currently the Dublin City Arts Officer.

The Off Broadway production drew over forty positive reviews including *Time Out New York:* "There is a great deal that is admirable about Tramway... Jermanok's simple direction is well tailored to the intimacy of the Chelsea Playhouse," and *The Wall Street Journal* which added: "Ray Yeates is doing a powerful solo turn in Dermot Bolger's *The Tramway End...* Mr. Yeates does give us something precious: the soul of a human being."

Over the course of the next few years, I had something like 529 meetings with producers, directors and investors in my home city New York, of course, as well as London, Paris, Berlin, Madrid, Istanbul, Boston, Toronto, Chicago, Miami, LA and San Francisco. In New York and in suburban Boston, I met with a wealthy investor who had an idea for setting a movie in New Bedford, the historic whaling city immortalized in Moby Dick. The place now often referred to as New Beige, because over seventy percent of its population is Portuguese. There are Portuguese bakeries, restaurants, nightclubs and musical venues where the soothing Fado music can be heard. Fado is essentially Portuguese blues, but it is a distinct form of music with a style and presentation of its own.

My brother Stephen and I signed a contract to write the script and soon we were researching this fascinating area of southern coastal Massachusetts that had not been host to a feature film for over seventy years. New Bedford is located in a region called the Gold

Coast which is about 30 miles west of Cape Cod without the hassle of traffic and congestion. The Gold Coast also consists a number of beautiful coastal towns like Marion, Mattapoisett, Fairhaven, Dartmouth and Westport—to name a few.

Research is amazingly underrated. Whether you are researching the artistic or business side of your craft, it can be transformative. It certainly was in our case. We were down for a week or so and started checking out everything that is Portuguese. Many of the characters were inspired by actual people we met at Portuguese grocery stores, restaurants and the like. The most defining moment came when we went to a low-key restaurant and heard a Fado singer perform. The soul stirring music mesmerized us. We were in shock when we first heard this Fado singer perform. Our souls were indeed ignited. We decided then and there to have one of our lead characters be a Fado singer.

We went back several times to the Gold Coast and New Bedford to interview, watch, and interact with the Portuguese and their community. My company was almost perfect. My brother Stephen is the greatest guy in the world and one helluva writer. When writing screenplays, we really seem to compliment one another literarily. As a superb journalist, he is exceptional at story and structure. With my theater and acting background, I am adept at characters and dialogue. There was eventually a long article about our screenwriting process in Script Magazine.

We both share a love of travel and have been to almost one hundred countries combined. The interesting ethnic elements of our developing story, namely Portuguese music, culture, cuisine were intriguing to us because we both have a fascination with the planet and culture. When he is not writing or directing with me, my brother is one of the top travel writers in the world and also has an expert travel blog and travel agency, www.activetravels.com.

However close they are, two grown men in each other faces

for a long period of time can be nerve-wracking. I remember we were doing research for "Passionada" on the cobbled streets of New Bedford near their famed Whaling Museum. I vaguely recall that we still had more research to do, but Steve suddenly pivoted and turned toward his loving and then very young family. He had unilaterally and abruptly declared that he was out of there. One thing led to another and suddenly these two human whales, the Jermanok Brothers, were wrestling on those now dangerous cobbled New Bedford streets. We soon came to our senses and decided to properly communicate like mature adults. Thank God, it was not an omen.

We finished the first draft of the script in a few months. Our financier seemed very happy but had some notes that we naturally tried to accommodate. Finally, we had a working draft, but the financier cum producer needed my co-producing help. We tried to direct the film, but he wanted someone who had previously directed multiple films to great acclaim. It was not easy to find an acclaimed director to direct someone else's romantic comedy script for some reason, but I stumbled on a director, Dan Ireland, who had directed a sensational film, "The Whole Wide World" about the 1930's pulp writer who created "Conan the Barbarian. The film is one of my favorites and was nominated for a host of awards. It also starred Vincent D'Onofrio and discovered the then unknown Renee Zellweger.

Dan loved the script and signed on. We were soon close friends. Within two years of writing "Passionada," we had the rare experience of being on the set of the film in New Bedford and the Gold Coast of Massachusetts. New Bedford went crazy over the opportunity to host a film. The whole city was very enthusiastic and supportive. We tried to use as many local residents for cast and crew as we could. I really loved being there. There were the typical production ups and downs; the controlled chaos of completing the production of a feature film, but that is for another book perhaps.

I'm very proud of "Passionada"—it's a real sweet crowd

pleaser. It went on to premiere at a dozen film festivals. It was the closing night film of the prestigious Seattle International Film Festival and received "Two Thumbs Up" from the late legendary film critic, Roger Ebert, who also reviewed it upon its release in 2003-2004, when he stated, "The movie has been directed from a screenplay by the brothers Jim and Steve Jermanok, whose freelance writing credits sound like homework for this story. Steve wrote the book 'New England Seacoast Adventures,' and here the brothers create an emotional adventure for a down-and-out gambler and a Portuguese-American widow who sings of lost love and vows she will never marry again."

We had an amazing premiere at LA's huge Arclight Theater with red-carpet paparazzi and dozens of movie stars. A particular highlight was when Preston Sturges, Jr., the son of the acclaimed screenwriter and director that greatly inspired the work of Stephen and I, introduced himself and told us how much he enjoyed the film. The next day, we had a review from *The LA Times* film critic Kevin Russell that we couldn't have written ourselves for fear of being delusional. In it, he writes: "The Jermanoks strive for and achieve a romantic comedy with humorous, fanciful plotting yet shaded by genuine tenderness and passion...Writers Jim and Stephen Jermanok intricately yet briskly bring Celia and Charlie together." That was a very joyous day. The next week, famed film critic Rex Reed added in *The New York Observer*, "Passionada is a charming and luxurious romantic interlude carefully constructed and greatly enhanced by fresh dialogue."

The New Bedford premiere was attended by over 3,000 people. There was a press conference that went on for two hours followed by an extraordinary speech, in my humble opinion, by the then Mayor, Frederick M. Kalisz Jr., who thanked the parents of the Jermanok Brothers for "raising two fine boys who have given so much pride to our community." It doesn't get better than that. I was so pleased that my late dad, Julius Jermanok, was in attendance.

Our sophisticated romantic comedy was released in over 120 American cities in 2003-2004 by Samuel Goldwyn Films. It screened theatrically in the New Bedford area for over a year. It was later released in 2004-2005 by Columbia Tri-Star in over 150 countries worldwide. The film stars: Jason Isaacs (Lucius Malfoy in the "Harry Potter" films, "The Patriot"), Academy Award nominee Seymour Cassel, Theresa Russell ("Black Widow"), Sofia Milos ("CSI: MIAMI") and introduced the then virtually unknown Emmy Rossum (Showtime's "Shameless," "Phantom of the Opera"). With a phenomenal soundtrack by Harry Gregson-Williams ("Shrek" "Chronicles of Narnia") the film still brings tears to my eyes whenever I see it.

A few years later, my brilliant San Francisco-based filmmaker friend Tony Barbieri called me about a recent script he completed entitled "Em," which he wanted me to produce. The film is a romantic drama about two twenty-somethings who fall in love and live together. Soon, Amanda or "Em," played by Stef Willen in her first feature film role, starts displaying symptoms of mental illness. Her boyfriend Josh (Nathan Wetherington) tries his best to keep the relationship going.

Tony burst onto the independent film scene in 1998 when his film "One" appeared at the Sundance Film Festival, where it was praised by audiences and critics alike. It was nominated for an Independent Spirit Award. Barbieri's second feature film, "The Magic of Marciano," starring Nastassja Kinski and Robert Forster also drew universal praise in 2000. We both enlisted one of the finest film composers in the world, Harry Gregson-Williams to score and produce "Em" with me. As always, Harry was exceptional.

Tony succeeded at making a compelling and moving film that many have described as "the most and raw and authentic film about mental illness in the past 25 years." Needless to say, I'm very proud of it, particularly when those who have been affected by mental illness tell me that "Em" has provided them with comforting solace.

"Em" had its world premiere at the Seattle International Film Festival, where it won the Grand Jury Prize. It went on to win the Criterion Collection's International Inspiration Award, The International Film Guide Award, Best Film at the Strasbourg International Film Festival and Best Producer Award at the Brooklyn International Film Festival. It was released in late 2011 by SnagFilms and Vanguard Cinema.

I also managed to direct a documentary, helped to start a small entertainment agency, write and direct several commercials, industrials, and web series. I love wearing a number of hats, maybe too many, as I find the variety stimulating. It also eases my stress of making a living creatively—which I have done for over 25 years. I write, direct and produce in films, theater, TV and new media. When waiting for my next feature to be financed, I really enjoy making short films as it keeps me in practice.

While it is important to have expertise in one or even two occupations, **it is equally important to be as versatile as you possibly can—in every which way**. Those artists and filmmakers who restrict themselves to one medium or one location may eventually find themselves without work. Be flexible and open to experiencing other occupations, mediums and locations. Be open to all opportunities.

Work begets work. Always welcome an occupational challenge because you never know where it can lead you. The people you will meet in one medium may lead you to job opportunities in another medium. You may have a specific vision for your career, but sometimes it takes a life of its own. Allow it to take its course. Try to learn as much as you can about other options than those you planned for. These other options, at times, may become your only options. In other words, always be hungry for opportunities, knowledge and experience.

* * *

REFINING YOUR CRAFT

I understand you completely. I really do. You think that because you picked up this book, you simply need some insight into the business side of being creative. You have achieved success in your craft and want even more. You are ready to get to that next plateau. "Oh, the craft... ," you say, "I have the craft down. Let's not go there, okay? I'm so, so ready." I am going there. You could not be more wrong.

Generally speaking, this business is much, much more competitive that you can imagine. **That is, there are more competitors than you think and they may be much more gifted than you currently believe**. Does that mean you should hang up your tutu and run home? NO. It also doesn't mean that you should run blindly into a tornado. You need to learn all you can about that tornado, and we'll discuss it throughout this treatise. But I just want you to be realistic about the market for your craft or art—and how damn good you need to be to succeed.

Both Robert DeNiro and Al Pacino take part in acting classes and private coaching when they are "at liberty" between films. So does Nicole Kidman and J Lo and many others who understand that whatever their status or level, they need to keep their creative instrument in tune.

It is absolutely essential that you practice, practice and practice and keep learning and improving. Believe me, many of your competitors are enhancing their craft. What about you? Avoid any excuse or rationalization that allows you to stop practicing. Never ever rest on your laurels. Never focus solely on making a living creatively. Sure, it's the purpose of this book after all, but you cannot neglect your craft for any reason or serious length of time. If you do, you run the risk of making yourself less of a contender for that next job or creative livelihood, for that matter. Remember what Marlon Brando said On the Waterfront "I could've been a contender. I could've been somebody... " Don't let this happen to you.

Whether you're an actor, writer, filmmaker, or artist of any stripe, you want to create your luck. Luck has been described as being in the right place at the right time. A few rare souls have a real knack for this. I'm really not sure if this is under our control. Luck also has a more proactive definition as initially stated by the mid 1st century Roman philosopher, Seneca, who said, "Luck is what happens when preparation meets opportunity." The auditions, competitions, meetings with investors, directors, art gallery owners, record executives and other opportunities will arise in your life. The key is to be prepared for them and the best way to do that is to always be in tiptop creative shape.

I have had the occasion to encounter numerous creatives (many of whom have achieved some success in their fields), who have the notion that practicing and improving is beneath them. That they simply don't need to practice unless the business calls for it. Unless they have a job or are getting paid for it. Hogwash. This is simple self-sabotage. You can always get better. You can always IMPROVE.

The most successful artists are always working to perfect their craft. They are in a continuing process to improve. They are also skilled at being self-critical without being self-defeating. They analyze their game and discern their strengths and weaknesses. Make no mistake, these strengths should not be ignored. They should be practiced, finely tuned and improved.

The weaknesses should be the focus of intense analysis and exercise. What are your weaknesses? How are you going to address them? Successful creatives are not afraid to figure out their weaknesses. Once diagnosed, they work hard to build up those creative muscles.

Versatility can make the difference. When you meet or perform for a rep or gatekeeper, you never know what skill or work they may be seeking. They may be looking for a creative who has the exact talents you neglected. That is why it is important to work on your versatility. One way of doing this is to **stretch yourself artistically**. Be completely honest with yourself and assess the current status of your craft. Now speak to your instructors, experts, friends and peers in your field. Ask them to be candid. What do they think are your biggest strengths or weaknesses? Where are the area(s) for improvement in your craft? Now that you have done the necessary research, don't be depressed or discouraged. Now is the time to work hard.

When you focus on those parts of your craft that need improvement, stretching by building bigger artistic muscles, you will be amazed at the progress you can make. Generally, it is just a matter of attention, time and training.

Don't be afraid to take classes, workshops or webinars that teach or emphasize the creative skills that require attention. Clear the cobwebs now! Clean out your craft closet. It may be difficult at first, but simply begin the process. As Woody Allen exclaimed, "Ninety percent of life is just showing up." Be willing to show up and focus on your weaknesses! That's it. When you do so, it can be a joy to realize rapid improvement. You may even discover a strength that you didn't think you possessed or better yet, a completely new focus for your craft. Either way, refining your craft makes you a lot more marketable.

Use Your Life. Whether you are an actor or a writer any other type of craftsperson, you have an ever-present goldmine at your disposal and it's called your life. You'd be surprised how underused this vein of knowledge and direction is, but I assure you it is. Many artists simply don't want to go there. I beckon you: GO THERE!

Are you using life experiences to inform and better your craft? Have you canvassed your social, emotional, occupational and geographic histories and experiences in your craft? I urge you to do so as it can only open doors (do I sound like Freud here?), enhance and enliven your work.

My friend Spalding Gray was the best storyteller or monologist I've ever seen. In his life and art, he treated everyone like they were his personal therapist. To hang out with him in public was a real treat to see how fast he connected with complete strangers. He was absolutely open, candid and uncensored in this way. His performances were riveting—the entire adult audience were quickly transformed into five year olds staring at their local librarian turning the pages of a spellbinding book.

Spalding's performances led to such acclaimed films as "Swimming to Cambodia," "Monster in a Box," and "Gray's Anatomy". Spalding Gray's work is an extreme example of a craftsman drawing upon their life. The strictly autobiographical route. I can't say I recommend this.

It may not be necessary to be so directly autobiographical. When my co-writing brother Stephen and I wrote our film script for "Passionada," we were writing about a love story which takes place in the Portuguese community of New Bedford, Massachusetts. This former whaling town was the setting for Melville's classic Moby Dick. The population of New Bedford, or as the natives call it New Beige, is seventy percent Portuguese. "Passionada" became the first American film to primarily focus on the Portuguese immigrants in America. Stephen and I didn't know squat about the Portuguese. We are not Portuguese and knew very few Portuguese. Sure I had been to Portugal, but then I was thinking about beaches, food and wine--if I was thinking at all.

Stephen and I needed to do extensive research on the area and it helped us enormously to come up with our story and characters. But we also used our lives. We used what we know. We were both raised in Schenectady in upstate New York, which is still predominantly Italian and Polish. I am also a longtime resident of Astoria, Queens in New York City, which is predominantly Greek. Although neither of us had any experience living with the Portuguese, there was a long history with Italian, Polish and Greek communities. It turns out that all of these ethnic groups share common values: namely the devotion to family, church, and hard work. They all celebrate vibrant cultures and cuisines as well.

So we used our lives—that is we used our life experiences living with these three ethnic groups to inform our craft: to write about the Portuguese.

Again, it doesn't have to be strictly autobiographical. It can be indirectly autobiographical, but your life and personal history can be enormously effective in making your craft come alive. Making you better at what you do. Try not to close that door. Dig deep and go there, baby. You never know what riches you'll find.

God is in the details. I like this line, which I have used in promotional or marketing discussions. I use it here because it applies to your artistic craft as well. The competitiveness of our industry demands that you pay attention to every detail of your creative career including the artistic craft itself. Are you doing all you can to practice your craft? What can you do to improve? Are you taking advantage of all the expert instruction available in literature, classes and on the Web? Everything you do in this regard will help to give you a competitive edge, which could be the deciding factor in whether you make a living creatively.

The following are my two cents of wisdom for several creative careers. If your career is not specified here, try to apply this advice to your particular goals. After all, in creative careers as well as humanity, we are much more alike than different. Once again, you need to build all your creative muscles to the best of your abilities. All the creative weapons at your disposal. Need another metaphor? I think not.

Actors. Not only is it important way to keep in artistic shape, but a regular acting class can serve other purposes. It can provide priceless information about auditions, agents and managers. It can provide you with friends and allies pursuing the same career goals. It is also a wonderful way to stretch yourself without professional consequences. Get professional feedback from your teachers and peers. Listen to what they say, but don't feel compelled to take all of it. Use what rings true and disregard the rest. A lot of acting teachers think they are gurus. This is usually nonsense. Real life gurus in any subject are extremely rare if not nonexistent. **Use what rings true to you and disregard the rest**.

It's all about booking jobs. Actors often do very well at auditions and get very close, but they don't book the job. The casting director offers praises them like crazy, but again, nada. This can be awfully frustrating.

The answer may well be taking a good **Audition Technique** class. There is a major difference between acting and auditioning. They are completely different creative muscles. Some great actors can't audition if their life depended on it, but succeed somehow in spite of their shortcoming. You don't have this luxury. It is incumbent upon you to work on your auditioning technique via a great audition class. Do the necessary research and find the best teacher in your area and enroll.

A great voice class can also spell the difference, particularly if you are a singer or need to project a stronger voice. If you're acting in a country other than where you were born, don't be stubborn—try taking lessons with an accent reduction teacher. It may prove to be life and career transforming.

Monologues. The use of monologues has been on the decrease in favor of interviews or cold readings, but here are some guidelines:

- Pick a monologue less than two and a half minutes. Casting directors generally have deficient listening skills and adolescent attention spans. Less is definitely more.
- Avoid selecting an overused monologue. These monologue clichés can be incredibly boring for casting directors. Don't forget—you can source your piece from theater as well as films, novels, short stories. If you happen to be a great scribe, even something you write for yourself.
- Monologue selection is everything. The right piece can make an average actor shine and the wrong piece can dampen a superb actor. Find a piece that has the *capacity to impress*. In other words, if you do it well, you can hit it out of the park. Lest you forget, that is your goal: to *impress* the casting director. A piece with more than one color (mood or beat) is particularly useful because it shows your versatility and chops.
- Be ready and open to be directed. Especially if you're performing for a director. Guess what? They like to direct. How directable are you? You must always be able to make adjustments, however slight. The most directable actors work the most.
- It must be you. Make sure the monologue is something realistic for your type. It fits your age, gender, personality, occupational and ethnic range. A role for which you could easily be cast. A role that could be written for you.

Paid auditions. In major cities, there is an opportunity to take paid auditions. These are "paid auditions" or meetings with professional casting directors, agents or managers. I don't have any objection to these although they are a bit exploitative. However, I have known actors to get representation and book jobs through these. Just don't overdo it—maybe 1-3 per month. Tops. After all, it is in your best interests to meet as many **Primary Contacts** or individuals who can represent, hire, or invest in you. You have to meet most of these people anyway. Make sure to be very selective in choosing your paid auditions and do the necessary research to determine who are best for you to meet given your level and type. And always ask for honest feedback when you're done. For more info, check the **Art of Schmoozing Chapter**.

Writers. Yes, writing gurus do exist. Sometimes, they're even worse than acting gurus. Please see the comments above. Take what is useful and disregard the rest. Writing workshops, retreats and webinars can be very useful to improve your craft. Try to research the one that best suits you.

Using your genre and understanding the rules of your genre can be the key to success. Make an honest assessment of your work. **Pick the genre that you're best at compared to your professional peers, not necessarily your favorite genre**. If you write in more than one genre, pick the one that is currently the most commercial and make it your **primary genre**. Focus on this genre first and foremost. When you have done all you can in service of your **primary genre**, you can use the remaining time to pursue your **secondary genres**. This will help guide your writing craft and will help you to stratify and market yourself.

It may be possible that you picked the wrong genre, that is, a genre that is not working for you. Have you given it enough time? Stand back and relax. Evaluate. Don't be afraid to experiment with another genre if you are certain that your **primary genre** is not working.

In addition to genre selection, another common problem is selecting the wrong writing medium. This is a very delicate subject, because I never want to encourage you to quit anything ever. But if your current medium is not serving your career, think about trying something else. In other words, if years of screenwriting is not making you money, what about writing a novel? If dialogue is your thing, maybe authoring a play is the way to go. If journalism is getting you down, what about writing a whole non-fiction book about a subject that turns you on. Be open to trying another medium if the first choice ain't working.

Writing habits. Discipline is key. If you want to be a writer, WRITE. If you already are a writer, WRITE. Try to do it everyday. Set a certain time. The same time everyday. Some writers do it very early because they may hold down a 9-5 job. Scott Turow of Presumed Innocent fame writes everyday before he commutes to his daily grind as a practicing lawyer. The late mega-bestselling author Michael Creighton would wake up at the ungodly hour 4 o'clock in the morning when he was in the thick of writing a novel. I don't think I've ever been awake at that time—outside of my dark bathroom. It doesn't matter when—just make sure to do it everyday.

Don't be afraid to spit out that first draft. In screenwriting circles, it can be known as the "vomit draft." Write fat. That is, overwrite a little bit. Then sculpt it down in the rewrite stage. Everyone has their own writing system. What is yours? The best writing evolves from editing and rewriting. These are definite skills in their own right. You can always shape things later, but first things first, get out that first draft.

Join or form a writers group. It can be an organized group like a meetup group or you can form a group made up of your friends or peers--it doesn't really matter. It can be formal or informal. Try to insure that your fellow writers are of the highest caliber possible. This may seem daunting at first, but over time and a minimum of networking, a high quality group will eventually evolve. Another essential quality is that your fellow writers will give open and honest feedback in the most detailed, specific way possible. Platitudes are from mom, not fellow writers.

Often, we are too close to the literary forest to see the trees. Drat, did I just butcher another idiom? Having the writers you respect give their input can be invaluable and can potentially transform your rewrite into something much better and more marketable/sellable. For every screenplay and book I write, I always send my stuff to a small, select group for their opinion. Not only are they a necessary sounding board but they also provide a layer of self-protection before my work is seen by the all-powerful **Primary Contacts**--reps and buyers. You know, the agent, manager, producer, director, publisher and the like. If my group approves my work, I send it on. They serve as my internal green light, if you will.

No second chance! There is another damn good reason to send your literary genius to your writing cadre. If your work is not ready and the all-powerful professionals read it and are not impressed— there is no second chance! Do you understand?? Unless you have achieved huge success in the past, chances are they will never look at a second or subsequent draft.

I understand, you may be eager to show your work to the world. I get it. You've worked for three or four months on a screenplay or years on a play or novel, and you want to get it out to the world. This is perfectly natural, and I want you to get it out there as much as you possibly can. But please hold back on getting to those professionals who can rep you or hire you until your work is exceptional. Don't blow your opportunity—make sure it is ready to be seen by a very busy and jaded elite. This goes double for actors and artists by the way. Make sure your work is the absolute best it can be before you present it to those professionals who can impact your life.

Give birth already. Notwithstanding the previous paragraph, another common problem is to be too tough on yourself. That is, you refuse to get your work out there after years—in front of those professionals who can help make it a reality. This may sound like a contradiction to the above, but it is not. This is naked self-sabotage.

You may think you don't have the talent or your work is not ready and never will be ready. Try to find or form a group of fellow writers so they can check it out. Do a rewrite or two--and then give birth already! Your work will never live if it suffocates in your hard drive or desk drawer. Maybe the professional elite will reject you, but that's okay. The power of the literary agents, publishers and gatekeepers is fading. Now you have options that never existed years ago. You can create your own audience, self publish, create an eBook, put on a play or complete a low budget film. If you don't try, you'll never know.

Filmmakers. Once again, there has never been an easier time to make a short or film. Don't allow indie or studio gatekeepers, name stars, producers or investors hold you back or delay you in any way. Keep on approaching those who can represent or hire you, but always try to be working on films. It is less expensive than ever before to make a short or webisode or even a feature. There are thousands of features that are made nowadays for less than 100G or even 50G. Whatever the budget or lack thereof, the filmmaking experience and on-the-job training will make you a much better filmmaker. You will also discover and refine the perfect crew and cast to work with. When the big opportunity comes, you will be much better prepared to make your own luck.

Stratify. It is extremely important to stratify yourself in the film world. What genre(s) and budgets ranges are you focusing on? This will help you to narrow down the vast film world. It will make it easier and more manageable for you to pursue professional film work. You never want to be in the position of pitching a 500G horror film to a producer who only makes $100 million sci-fi films. Stratify and specify! Make sure you're meeting the people that are right for you and your needs. Those who could finance or help the specific projects you want to make. When you have chosen your strata, it also makes it easier to find those who eventually help you market and distribute your film—that is, if you choose not to do it yourself.

Don't put all your eggs into one project. One of the most common mistakes that filmmakers can make is having too few projects. Think about having projects in differing budget ranges, genres and mediums. This way, you're prepared when you meet a rep or buyer who already has a low budget drama feature or reality show about fortune hunters. Or when you meet the producer/investor who detests horror films or musical theater. Does that mean that you tuck your tail between your legs and walk away? Does that mean that you begin to ask them about their recent awards or next travel adventure? No, although bonding is always important. Now is the time to whip out your other project. Ta-da, look what I have—your favorite genre, a romantic comedy. In meetings, don't pitch more than two or three projects at a time. Film or theater producers/investors may pretend they can handle more, but they can't.

Artists. Get some studio space of your own and practice, practice, practice. Do it everyday. Are you working fast enough? Most artists are much more versatile than they think. Don't be afraid to experiment with new mediums or styles. Or even colors, for that matter. Mix it up! It may just be a question of a slight adjustment, which you should not be too stubborn to implement. Don't be too stubborn to compromise. You never know the one piece that will click with gallery owners or collectors. It is important to also stratify yourself in this field. Are you promoting yourself in the right way? Are you marketing to the right galleries or collectors? Would your efforts be more successful in another city or country? Be open to making the necessary adjustments to determine your artistic and commercial groove.

Make It Happen! Whatever your art, talent or passion, don't ever let reps, buyers, casting directors, production executives, investors or other forms of gatekeepers stop or discourage you. Avoid solely depending or relying on them. They are very important to know, of course, and this book has devoted many chapters to this. But you must keep doing your craft everyday. Or as much as you can manage. If you don't have a coach verbally whipping you, be your own coach! Set aside time to be as disciplined as you possibly can. Turn off the phone and avoid the texts and emails. Push yourself to do the best work you possibly can.

Conclusion. There may be some growing pains in learning your craft or learning to make it happen for you. Don't be intimidated by this, but rather be excited by the challenge. Don't be hesitant to take classes, workshops or webinars to stretch yourself or to strengthen your weak spots. Stop worshipping gurus—take what you can away from them and disregard the rest. Try to utilize those creative friends and peers you respect bigtime. Get their advice to evaluate the quality of your latest work. They may not be right all the time, but if enough of them are giving you similar advice or notes, take it seriously. Again, use what makes sense and disregard the rest.

Does it make sense to partner with another creative professional or form a group? It could make things easier for you than always fighting the good fight by yourself. It's also great to have a teammate to help you cushion all the blows and rejections our business has to offer. **It's never been easier or cheaper to create, build an audience, publicize, market and distribute your work. Take the leap now!**

* * *

WATCH MY BACK:
FINDING YOUR CREATIVE FAMILY

To most people in the outside world, trying to make a living creatively is a crazy pursuit. Why would anyone subject themselves to a stream of unimaginable odds, obstacles and rejections? Why would any poor soul subject himself or herself to such an uphill battle? That's easy to address. <u>Because that's who we are</u>.

My own parents certainly couldn't believe it when I began my own creative quest. I was fortunate to receive great grades in high school and college, particularly in math and sciences. They tried to convince me to get a graduate degree of some type to fall back on. "What's wrong with my undergraduate degree?" I responded. But they would not take no for an answer. My mother Beverly was a guidance counselor for over forty years at Albany High School in upstate New York, where she helped thousands of underprivileged students get into college. Whenever I came home from Cornell, there would be stacks and stacks of law school applications begging for my attention on the wooden staircase leading to my attic-turned-bedroom.

Most parents who are not creative or haven't tried to realize their creative dreams will simply not understand what the hell you are doing. They will probably think it is an enormous waste of abilities that can be applied to conventional occupations. Especially those that offer steady paychecks and financial security. Parents know the odds are not stacked in your favor and may try to get you to commit to a set period of effort like three or five years. Most creatives I know who have abided by such a term have not made the cut. I don't know why exactly, but maybe there is a danger that it becomes a self-fulfilling prophecy when you know you have a time safety net. Although in the weak present economy, I understand the impulse. Indeed, it may be a sage precaution.

If your family and friends don't quite understand your creative pursuit, persist in going for it--but try to educate your *civilian* or uninformed parents, siblings and friends about the difficulty journey ahead. Teach them about the training and tenacity that is required. Let them know about the various stages of typical creative career paths and how they can differ. Invite them to all of your performances, shows and openings. Ask for their support! Trust me, you'll need all the support you can muster.

Maybe you're one of the lucky few whose parents can financially and emotionally support your creative endeavors. Yippee! Let them know what the costs are and how important training, mentorship and knowledge are to becoming a creative success. Always ask for their advice when you stumble artistically or personally. Keep your loved ones informed of all the victories however minor you may perceive them to be. Such victories don't come around too often—make sure you relish and cherish them.

Your Creative Family. Whether or not you are able to draw support from your family and friends, you will need to form a supportive family of your own—your creative family. A group of fellow creative professionals who you trust and respect.

A cadre of friends and peers who bring out the best in you. Those folks who know why you are special and really get you. They will prove to be a Godsend in so many ways.

Be very selective about who you choose to be in **your creative family**. If you make certain they are talented, open and honest, they can really make you and your work better. Your creative family can help you gauge what level you have attained in your craft. They can help you to improve and advance your talent. As fellow creative professionals, they have the background and expertise to truly evaluate your acting, writing, art or music. Don't be afraid to let them do this for you. They must be genuinely honest in their critiques of your Shakespearean monologue, dark comedy script or Off Broadway lead role. Most important, they can support you, comfort you and pick you up off the ground when times are rough. And believe me, there will be rough times.

Don't be afraid to include your real family creatively if the shoe fits. Whether it's practice or work—they can be your perfect partners. There's a reason why so many brothers form writing and directing duos. They can be candid with one another. There is usually a strong mutual trust. Not to mention a creative shorthand or private vocabulary. They won't be shy about letting you know if you come up short. On the other hand, they'll be the first to slap you five when you kick ass. They keep your game up and you never want to let them down. After all, they are family. Remember that Sister Sledge song "We Are Family?"

Nothing makes me happier to work with my creative or real family, whatever the medium. Some of the best moments of my career have been working (writing and directing) with my brother Stephen. I still remember his shocked face as the Mayor of New Bedford, Massachusetts praised us at the "Passionada" premiere before thousands of appreciative locals.

Your creative family is even more essential for surviving the hard knocks this business delivers on an all too frequent basis. Isolation sucks. At least it does for this social New Yorker. Pursuing a creative career can be damn lonely. Even if you're not a social animal, having a creative family is akin to having a nurturing support group available 24-7. There is always someone there for you who can commiserate with you about your latest trials and tribulations-- with an awareness that your noncreative family lacks. Just being able to speak with someone about the excitement and letdowns of your career is an incredible source of comfort.

Coping with rejection. Our business is like no other. The ups and downs, the joys and disappointments are a continual if not daily part of our lives. Particularly the rejections, oh the rejections. They never seem to stop. They can take numerous forms whatever your creative field of endeavor. But you don't get them if you don't try— so that is not the answer, my friend.

From the day my acclaimed journalist brother Stephen was starting out, he saved all the rejection letters he received from newspapers, magazines and publishers. Now the folder is colossal, like three or four inches thick. When he addresses beginning writers, he never fails to bring out this dog-eared folder. Audiences love it, especially the form letter rejection from Mad Magazine, which simply read: "It didn't tickle our funny bone." They suddenly grasp how normal and routine these rejections are. They learn to never ever take these rejections personally. **To take rejection personally is a recipe for failure.** If you try to make a living creatively, you should expect to be rejected countless times during the course of your career.

The question is how do you cope with the rejections that come your way? Learning to cope with rejection can make the difference in determining whether your creative career succeeds or fails. When practicing your craft, it important to be sensitive. Indeed, the vast majority of creatives have heightened sensitivity. However, when doing the necessary business and marketing to pursue a creative livelihood--you must develop thick skin--think rhinoceros thick. Let the rejections and negative encounters come and go. Like tears off a monkey's back. Never allow these to slow or stop you. Keep on going! Overcome all obstacles that get in your way. Even too many animal metaphors.

One of the best ways to escape the "blahs" is to call upon your creative family. They know firsthand exactly what you are going through. After all, they are on the same playing field. They know how unfair and unjust the creative business can be. They also appreciate how good you are at what you do. Your creative brothers and sisters are there to support you whatever problem comes your way.

Like it or not, misery loves company. Your creative family can trade stories with you about that occasionally nasty casting director, director, producer agent or development executive. They know exactly how you feel when you are down and they know how to pick you up. But you can't do this if there is no creative family in your life. You need to find your own creative brothers and sisters with whom you can share creative paths. Start the process now and always keep your eyes open for new members. This is too hard of a journey to do all by your lonesome. Find your own creative family to grow with. They will be crucial to your artistic survival and eventual success.

* * *

DISTINGUISH YOURSELF!

You're one of kind, aren't you? So tell me why! There is no better predictor of success than how well you are able to distinguish yourself from the pack. What does this mean exactly? Of course, it is incredibly important to develop your craft. There is no better way to distinguish yourself than by your talents.

Dan Ireland, my close friend and acclaimed director of our film, "Passionada," loves to describe how he "discovered" Renée Zellweger when he was casting for his film directorial debut, "The Whole Wide World." "We were seeing hundreds of actresses for an important lead role that contained so many 'colors' of acting. But I thought using a well-known actress would detract from the audience's attention. For weeks and weeks, we auditioned one actress after another until Renée came and read. She had some small credits, but never carried a film before. Indeed, she was never cast in any role beyond that of a supporting role. I asked her to read a scene, then another, and yet another. Each time, she brought something completely unique and original to the text. She was the role—there was no one else like her. I couldn't stop thinking about Renée. Soon, I found myself passionately persuading the producer that she was the one." Renée was splendid in the film, which soon established her as one of the best actresses in the world.

Okay, talent can occasionally pave the way, but it is usually not talent alone, unfortunately. No, that would be far too easy. The entertainment and media world is far from a meritocracy. You must DISTINGUISH YOURSELF!!! How are you distinctive from other beautiful blonde 20-year-old actresses? How are you different from other black 35-year-old comedians? What separates you from the pack of other action screenwriters? Why does your book belong on top of the sludge pile despite hundreds of other twenty-something restaurant bloggers? How are your novels distinctive from other British mystery writers? How is your horror directing distinctive from other scary directors? How is your singing different than other mezzo sopranos in their 40s? Why should a curator come to your studio instead of thousands of other abstract artists? You get the picture?

You need to **distinguish yourself** and your work from the tens of thousands of your creative peers. You need to begin to separate yourself from the rest of the pack starting now!

From the early 1970's through the mid 80's, Dr. Deborah Tannen evolved from a graduate student at UC Berkeley into a well-respected Professor of Linguistics at Georgetown University. She wrote dozens and dozens of scholarly articles as well as a book here and there about her field of study. But she wanted more. She wanted to separate herself from the rest of the pack of linguistic professors in America. Indeed, she wanted to distinguish herself as a mainstream author. How could she achieve this? She thought long and hard about what it would take. And she thought she had it figured out. Deborah Tannen decided to apply her expertise and appeal to the reading masses who probably did not know linguistics (the scientific study of language) from a hole in the head.

In 1986, she wrote *That's Not What I Meant! How Conversational Style Makes or Breaks Relationships* about how conversation affects relationships. The book was widely praised but sold only modestly. At the time, I got her a few speaking gigs. Dr. Tannen then wrote another academic book while continuing to focus on how she could distinguish herself on an even grander scale. The answer was published in 1990 in the form of her breakthrough book, *You Just Don't Understand: Women and Men in Conversation*. The book made *The New York Times* Best Seller list for almost four years, including eight months as Number 1.

Deborah Tannen figured what was not on the bookshelves, what the best use of her knowledge could be and created her very own niche. She somehow transformed her specific, if not esoteric, academic expertise into popular culture stardom. Now Dr. Deborah Tannen ranks as the world's most famous linguist simply because she learned to master the art of Distinguishing Yourself.

You Are the Product. The arts, entertainment, and media worlds are tremendously competitive. I cannot stress this enough. There are millions of creative professionals striving for a limited number of paying spots or opportunities, if you will. There are only so many openings that our business will support. There are many alternatives to the traditional business approach to make your way, of course. However, **there is absolutely no formula to succeeding in our business**.

To make a living creatively usually requires **superb self-promotion**. In this case, **you are the product**. You need to learn and understand all you can about your product, aka yourself. How exactly are you distinctive? What are your specific strengths? What kind of competitive edge do you have over your peers? What other ways are you appealing to the **primary contacts**: representatives or buyers of your talents? How can you create the most buzz about yourself? Only when you carefully access your distinctive skills and talents will you be able to promote yourself in the most effective manner.

When it comes to promoting and marketing yourself, many falter for various reasons. Fight the tendency toward insecurity or lack of confidence. It may be difficult, but these weaknesses are definitely self-destructive and self-sabotaging. There may be a natural shyness or awkwardness that comes with pitching yourself as your only client. This is nothing but normal for many of us. But don't let that stop you.

Mutual Favor. Try to learn and understand how to distinguish yourself with ease. It is not merely a choice but a necessity. You need to believe in yourself if you want a fighting chance. Hopefully, you have talent and want to go for it. If you do indeed have talent, remember you are doing a favor for those you approach for help. Let that sink in for a moment. To know, to represent, and to hire you is of benefit to you and the reps or buyers of your talents. We're talking mutually beneficial here, you got it? It's a two-way street, and not just a needy artist asking for handouts. May this realization embolden you to approach as many people as you possibly can. And to inspire you to creatively and commercially distinguish yourself along the way.

If you were selling something beside yourself, you would most certainly know exactly how your product or brand was distinctive. Let's say you sold vacuum cleaners for a living. This was a rather popular profession for much of the 20th century. The best vacuum cleaner salespeople were those who knew their brand backwards and forwards and inside out. Their livelihood depended on this knowledge. They could answer any question about their brand of vacuum cleaner. They knew the strengths of their particular vacuum cleaner and could defend it in comparison with other vacuum cleaners. They could even espouse why their brand was superior to other brands. And they learned how to market, promote and sell their brand in a way that connects with the potential buyer—whatever their personality or needs What precisely does the buyer want? How do you convince the buyer or rep that you have the "goods?" These are all skills you need to learn in distinguishing yourself. But first, you must practice, practice, and practice.

Again, if you were selling vacuum cleaners, you would know why your brand is distinctive. In the same way, you must know why you are distinctive. It is absolutely essential to promoting and selling yourself. And making a living creatively.

Still unconvinced of how important it is to distinguish yourself? Let's take a look at a recent superstar, shall we? Lady Gaga. This singer catapulted herself to the top of the Billboard charts and started winning awards almost out of nowhere. But the back story here is quite common: she paid her dues. She developed, refined and improved her singing gifts for many years. From an early age, she figured out how to distinguish herself by establishing her own persona and, in her case, hundreds of costumes to support that persona. Oh, those costumes are ridiculous, crazy (now her butcher is suddenly her fashion designer, etc.), and beautiful--but they also are a powerful magnet for attention. Lady Gaga will never be confused with any other singer.

One could argue that a role model or predecessor for Lady Gaga was Madonna. Talk about distinguishing yourself. From the beginning, Madonna distinguished herself from other East Village female singers in the early 80s. Then, she learned to distinguish herself from other singers worldwide. Once again, her original and distinctive persona did the trick. But Madonna didn't become lazily complacent over the last quarter century. Instead, she continued to reinvent herself over and over again to maintain her changing worldwide audience. And she continues to do so. **Thus, distinguishing yourself is not only limited to the beginning of one's career, but can also be crucial throughout one's entire career.** Continually distinguishing yourself can dramatically punctuate your career. Those who are best at it tend to have the longest careers!

Separating yourself from the pack may not be simple, instantaneous or easy. It may take you a month or two if not a year to figure out how to take advantage of your distinctions. What exactly makes you different and appealing?? What makes you you? Some people are never able to capitalize on why they're special or different and their careers generally suffer as a result. Please don't fall into this trap. Spend a lot of time on this if you need to. Ponder, contemplate and cogitate—it's that important. And come up with something that will attract as much interest and attention as possible.

The Curse of the Multi-Talented. Why am I discussing this here? Because having multiple creative talents can lead you in too many directions at once. And this can interfere with, complicate, if not preclude you from Distinguishing Yourself! For those of you who are multi-talented, for those of you who are able to hyphenate or pursue several creative career paths at once, I sincerely applaud you. But I also empathize with you. Because herein lies a horrible curse. If you are pursuing more than one creative career direction at a time, you can easily sabotage yourself. That's right. You can actually cancel yourself out! Working on too many career pursuits at once can diffuse your focus and sabotage your primary career goals.

It's a bitter irony that those who may be the most talented or multi-talented may fail while those creatives who can only do one thing (and not necessarily that well) succeed because they have no distractions. They keep plodding along toward their goal and making progress, however slow or incremental. The multi-talented is not as assured because they are constantly shifting their attentions.

The same can be said for being too much of a generalist. Or for those who hate to be "pigeonholed." Pigeonholing is described as a "term used to describe processes that attempt to classify disparate entities into a small number of categories (usually, mutually exclusive ones)." I count myself as an esteemed member of this camp. I hate that our business tends to pigeonhole creative professionals. It is extremely unfair as many of us can do multiple things. We can write, direct and produce. We can act, sing and tell jokes. We can paint and sculpt. We can act, direct and paint. In short we can strive toward creative excellence in multiple directions. We can become the next Renaissance Women and Renaissance Men.

But the simple reality is: industry executives, gatekeepers and/ or representatives can't handle this. They want it easy. These buyers and sellers of creative talents generally want to take the easiest (some would argue laziest) or most efficient route to getting deals done.

Stars can get around this as evidenced by the preponderance of actors who, for example, now direct or sing in a band. But the powers-that-be can't be swayed for the rest of us. They don't want to take the time and attention to consider using non-stars in ways even slightly tangential to how they are creatively known (or pigeonholed) in the business. It requires a willingness to be open minded and creative in their already pressured daily routines.

More important, it requires risk—a very scary word to almost all those in positions of power. Particularly in a corporate, multinational monolith in a scary economic climate. The power elite or gatekeepers solely seek to maintain their power and don't want to take chances. Ever! Thus, it is still difficult for an actor, writer, or director to jump from television to film. And this is just one example of many.

Prioritize. There is, however, a solution for the multi-talented, hyphenates, the next Renaissance Women and Men, or the pigeonholed. The solution is quite simple: **Prioritize.** It's wonderful that you have such diverse and various talents and gifts, but make sure to focus first on what you are best at compared to your peers. Not necessarily what you like to do the most. I would love to write Oscar-winning films, but compared to other screenwriters, I am best at writing comedies and romantic comedies—which are seldom Academy Award contenders.

It is also important to know your first choice or **Primary Goal** for many other reasons. It is the most efficient way. You'll make much more progress. Be honest with yourself. REALLY HONEST. Self-honesty is never easy. What are you best at compared with other creatives in your game? If applicable, please lose the self-delusions fast. Make that first choice. It's not set in stone—you can always change and re-prioritize if necessary. Satisfy all the daily requirements of pursuing your **Primary Goal** before you spend time on your other career pursuits aka **Secondary Goals**.

Primary and Secondary Goals. It may be a difficult choice, but you need to choose that **Primary Goal**. Once you have done this and not put it off (procrastination can be so damn inviting) you know exactly what to focus on each day. If you're best at two pursuits equally (extremely rare), then pick the one that has more commercial potential. That's right--make it easy on yourself. It will indeed be a colossal challenge whichever path you choose.

When you have done what you need to do to pursue your **Primary Goal** each day, when you have made some progress in achieving your **Primary Goal**, then and only then are you ready to move on to your **Secondary Goals**.

I can not tell you how important it is to be organized in this way. Otherwise, the potential to diffuse your energy is very strong. Once again, you will expend energy in too many directions at once. Let's call it **Secondary Goal Paralysis**. Your focus will be continually scattered. You may not even be aware of it. Of course, once you achieve your Primary Goal, it becomes much, much easier to pursue success wearing other creative hats. Indeed, it may be the combination of your talents that really distinguish yourself. But first things first.

Distinguish Thyself: Promotional Materials. In order to distinguish yourself in the most effective way, you must create superb promotional materials. If you lack confidence in your eloquence or writing, then it is fine to recruit someone to help you. Not a problem. But please don't take forever to do this. Just get this stuff accomplished, okay? Once you get it done, revise, revise and revise. Then accept and use them like crazy. You can't use these enough because you are promoting, publicizing and creating buzz for a valuable product: YOU!!

Personal Rap. No matter what your career accomplishments thus far, you owe it to yourself to make this rap as interesting, humorous, and memorable as possible.

For those of you who are not playboys or hip hoppers, a rap can be defined as 1-2 engaging sentences you can pitch about your beloved product. Let's say you meet an important agent, manager, producer, investor, director or art gallery owner in an elevator. What will you say to them? What is your elevator pitch? Remember the Boy Scout's motto: Be Prepared.

Again, allow me to use my vacuum cleaner salesperson analogy if I may. Perhaps, I'm simply sublimating a need to clean my place right now.

If you were that vacuum cleaner salesperson, you would have a handful of various raps. You would have a rap for the closing door or reluctant customer, you would have a rap for furiously busy customer and you would have a rap for the slightly interested customer—to name a few. Knowing the personality of your potential customer dictates which approach and rap to use. Each of these raps would aid you, the salesperson, in closing a sale as soon as you can. Each rap would be succinct but also effective in answering the critical question: why is my vacuum cleaner distinctive?

Primary and Secondary Contacts. In the same way, you must create a rap for your product, as in you, that works. Unlike a vacuum cleaner salesperson, you may not have a hundred opportunities each day. In fact, you may have only several opportunities a month, if that. So you must practice it on family, friends and others before you try it on someone who counts. Someone who can make a big difference in your career. That is, **a Primary Contact as in someone who can represent, hire or invest in you.** Someone who knows a **Primary Contact** is what we call a **Secondary Contact. That is someone who is friends with or close to Primary Contacts.** If you sneaked into a Secondary Contact's smart phone or Outlook, you would find Primary Contacts. Get it? You're going to memorize these terms if it kills me.

Now your new personal rap doesn't need to be the first words you utter to a valued new connection. You should try to be as genuine and engaging as possible. But some time before that person excuses himself or herself and leaves the room, it would be great if you convey your personal rap. And hopefully get a phone number or email in return. After all, that's what you're trying to do.

Let's say you are an unrepresented or under-represented (your current reps are not making things happen!) action screenwriter and you meet a screenwriting (literary) agent at a cocktail party. Try to speak to that person no matter what. They could be a life changer. I'm not telling you how to socialize with people (in this chapter, anyway), but simply arming you with a prepared sentence or two about yourself. This is doubly important because no matter how eloquent you may be, when you meet someone who could change your life, it is natural to be nervous. You may even grow silent or freeze. With a prepared **personal rap**, now you have a verbal security blanket.

One rap example is: "I just married the only single female left in a primitive tribe that has never seen a plane before. And I wrote a comedy script about it!" Don't be afraid to use humor if it lends itself to your rap. Humor, when used effectively, is always the ideal connection between two people. Whatever your rap, just refine it until it is ready for public use. Then get it out there and unleash it on those you need to meet. But, once again, make sure it distinguishes you and your work!

Your personal rap does not have to be confined to adventures of your tongue alone. It should also be on hand and available as a written rap. Whether on your desk wall to utter on command, or in your computer to copy and paste for emails, keep it close. Ideally, it could be that first opening sentence leading to your very own **Personal Paragraph.**

Personal Paragraph. In the same way you created a Personal Rap, it is also necessary to create a compelling and engaging **Personal Paragraph** to use in letters, emails and texts. Your career accomplishments should determine whether it is a thin or thick paragraph. Humor should not be a goal here. Instead, write in a People Magazine-style hyperbole. As any successful journalist can attest, the opening sentence should be a grabber. "One of the most respected novelists in Maine…" or "The production designer for the following award-winning films…" or "Sam Smith is one sculptor you'll never forget…" or "Perhaps the most acclaimed jazz singer in Minneapolis…" Be bold!! Don't be afraid to use such an exaggerated or over-sweeping first sentence because you need to convince the reader (who may very well be jaded or ADD) to read to the rest of the paragraph or letter.

On the other hand, don't lie about your accomplishments or career history either. And don't add too much filler if you can help it. Try to be true to yourself in your writing. Get to the point as fast as you can. Whatever you do, don't bore the reader. Keep your writing genuine, authentic, and intriguing enough to compel the reader to act on your behalf. So that they meet, then represent, hire or invest in you! Three to six sentences, tops.

Now you have a **Personal Paragraph** that you can use in any written discourse. Like the rap, don't just thrust this out there alone or before everything else in your missive. Place it gently below several introductory and inviting sentences. Need another example? Okay. "Dear X, Frank Pompous suggested that I send you my latest script, BIG HUBRIS." Then add your Personal Paragraph. Well, let's hold on here. In this case, you would actually be well advised to also include a **Work Paragraph**.

Distinguish Thy Work. For most creatives, it is also important to create a **Work Paragraph** that you have on hand to send out whenever you send out your work via email or letter. This would be a bottom-line and bare bones description of why your work is distinctive. Do you remember this word? I thought you did. And also any other significant information about your work that you want your **Primary Contacts** or **Secondary Contacts** to know. Try to be stylish and memorable as you can. Try to make a connection with your reader if you can. This is vitally important because they receive this type of information much more frequently than you can imagine. You must manage to shine!

With these paragraphs, always *"Leave Them Wanting More."* That's right—the age-old show business idiom--which is still continually neglected by numerous speakers, performers, writers and directors. In other words, don't describe too much or give away the plot. Avoid the ending if you are a screenwriter. You are simply titillating the reader. Just enough to get their attention to read or watch your work in full. Or more importantly, meet you in person! And then, fingers crossed, help you progress to the next plateau.

Distinguish Yourself Bio. When I was an agent at ICM, I had occasion to read scores and scores of bios, which can be defined as brief (as in 1-4 pages) biographies of renowned creative celebrities. Almost all of these were written by the prominent (not to mention, expensive) entertainment Public Relations firms of the time. Like today, entertainment clients would pay these firms a monthly retainer ranging from 2-10 thousand dollars. Despite the steep cost, however, most of these bios were poorly written. There were typos and grammatical errors galore. I mean all over the place. Randomly selected high school seniors could have done a better job!

On top of this, most of these documents were written without regard to the ultimate intention: to get their client more work!! They frequently resembled an archival document that needed to be locked away at the Library of Congress; not on the desks of the easily distracted show biz power players who could rep, hire or invest in their client. Or they were written in that phony, fluffy, and definitely off-putting style reminiscent of the program for a black tie charity benefit. Other bios were written in a clunky, overstuffed way--as if they wanted to literarily jam in all the awards and credits the client ever earned without regard to the reader.

As you can imagine, I was the one stuck with having to revise and overhaul the bios of these renowned and famous clients. I think it is important to write your bio whatever your accomplishments so far. If you have an abundance of jobs and credits, then it will be easier. If not, don't sweat it. Simply describe whatever relevant experiences or credits you have thus far. It may not fill the page, but that's okay. You have to start somewhere.

Here are some of my major suggestions regarding your **Distinguish Yourself Bio**:

- Keep the length to one page. In this digital age and sea of data, all of our attention spans are rapidly shrinking.
- Make it as reader-friendly as possible. Not just a boring or stuffed list.
- As described above, write in a slightly hyped *People Magazine*-style.
- Grab them with a slightly hyped or sweeping opening sentence.
- Make sure it is distinctive from the bios of your specific peers!
- Make sure some of *you* is in there.
- Embellish as much as you can without lying.
- Define or qualify enough so your reader can comprehend. Clarity is all important.
- Don't be bogged down by too many dates and years. It is much more about the what" than the "when." Particularly if the "when" is ages ago.
- Use single space. If you fall way short of filling the page, then use double space.
- Remember: It is supposed to help you get work. Don't hide what you do!!
- **Bold** the major awards, accomplishments, or credits if you wish.

- Whether it is paragraphs or sentences within paragraphs, put the most impressive distinction first (e.g. awards, credits, theaters, magazines, newspapers, critics, etc.). In other words, put *The New York Times* before *The Des Moines Register*. Look, I happen to love Iowa (the nicest people in the world!), but a quote from the former impresses more than the latter—and you are trying to impress!
- Send it out to those relatives, friends and colleagues who can write really well. Get their honest feedback and criticism before sending it out to potential employers or agents/managers.
- Don't forget to include your college, graduate school, and place of residence. These simple (but bonding) associations could be the deciding factor in whether you are contacted.
- Keep your sentences relatively short and staccato like a typical excellent piece of journalism.
- Avoid filler, unnecessary information or facts, and run-on sentences.
- It is okay to refer to yourself as Mr. or Ms. if you wish.
- Revise this bio every year. Or whenever you have a new accomplishment of any note.
- Be careful about including future dates. Make sure to revise these often if you do.
- Make sure every member of your team (e.g. partner, agent, manager, publicist, producer, lawyer, business manager, etc.) has your most recent bio.
- Post the entire bio or relevant sections on all your social media sites.

Please forgive my immodesty in advance. Here is my most recent **Paragraph Bio**:

JIM JERMANOK

Jim Jermanok is an award-winning writer, director and

producer, creative success expert, consultant and speaker. Jim wrote and produced the highly acclaimed romantic comedy, "Passionada," which was released by Columbia Tri Star in over 150 countries. His latest film "Em" recently won the Grand Jury Prize at the Seattle International Film Festival and the Criterion International Inspiration Award. It was just released by Vanguard Cinema and SnagFilms. He is also active in theater, TV and New Media. Mr. Jermanok is a former ICM Agent who helped to represent Alan Arkin, Arthur Miller, Shirley MacLaine, Dudley Moore, Helen Hayes, and General H. Norman Schwarzkopf, among others. Jim also speaks and conducts workshops worldwide on the subject of his upcoming book, *BEYOND THE CRAFT: What You Need to Know to Make A Living Creatively,* as well as *Making Your Projects Happen: Successful Film/TV Producing and Financing* and *The Art and Business of Screenwriting*

Do you see how I utilized quotes and Italics? How I limited or tried to limit the information delivered? I could have easily added 5-10 more clients or more awards, but if my reading audience stops reading or absorbing my words, what is the point? The goal is to impress but also have it be fully read and absorbed.

Really put the required time into **Distinguishing Yourself!** It is not an area you rush. You need to produce the highest quality written and oral raps, personal paragraphs, work paragraphs and bios. Soon you will have all the requisite promotional materials and be prepared for any type of meeting, interview, audition, or correspondence. Whether your interaction is with a **Primary Contact** or **Secondary Contact**, whether in person, or via the phone or email, you are now equipped to proceed to the next step: getting that contact to help you in your career! If you reach out to enough contacts, guess what? Getting to that next creative career plateau may be just around the corner.

* * *

FAKE IT TIL YOU MAKE IT:
CONFIDENCE IS KING

Once I was waiting in the office of the head of production of a film studio. That's right, the studio head honcho. Numero uno. Talk about butterflies. I was trying to prepare myself, compose myself, to freaken calm down in order to pitch a film project starring Ben Kingsley. We didn't have a script yet, but had a great treatment about an amazing but forgotten historical figure. A once renowned and fascinating performer from the turn of the century. After an interminable wait, I was finally led into a colossal office by a woman who clearly missed her calling as a global supermodel.

Following an exchange of initial pleasantries, I was urged to begin my pitch. All modesty aside, I hit it out of the park. I was Lawrence Olivier in Hamlet. The production head was mesmerized. "I had no idea this man existed. Is there a book?" I told him there were several, but not exactly bestsellers. In fact, they were actually very hard to obtain. The studio head told me he loved it but wanted Johnny Depp in the lead role. I love Johnny Depp but, at the time, I was loyal to my partner on the project, Mr. Kingsley, who had helped to organize this exact meeting.

Then the studio head proceeded to change the subject from my career to his. That is, from my proposed film to his upcoming slate of films. Quite a difference, eh? He was choosing which of the hundreds of films they had in development to greenlight or commence financing. To my astonishment, he wanted my opinion. He uttered the loglines of four or five possibilities and wanted me to choose my favorite. Why did he ask a complete stranger for input on a multi-million dollar decision? Because he wasn't sure. Maybe he was clueless or maybe he just wanted confirmation on a decision he had already made. Who knows? But one thing is certain: this studio head was insecure.

Insecurity is absolutely rampant in the creative world. If a random studio head is insecure, you can be damn sure the vast majority of creatives and creative executives are also insecure. Yes, that famous actor, director or singer that you admire. Even that well- known mogul who always looks so cocksure at the Sun Valley conference. From studio heads and movie stars to struggling writers and directors, from talent agency heads to indie producers, from the CEO of global conglomerates to aspiring songwriters, the creative lot is predominantly insecure. This is something to keep in mind if you ever find yourself being intimidated by the famous or successful in our business. This is also something to remember if you are ever insecure. You are in tremendous company.

The basis for this insecurity is manifold. One merely has to understand the uncertainty of the entertainment, media and arts world. It is an incredibly imperfect, unfair, erratic and unpredictable business. Such an arena will make almost any thinking person insecure. For both creatives and executives, success can be elusive for no apparent basis. Once it is obtained, success can wilt away for a long list of reasons. There is virtually no job security whatsoever. Standard business logic is frequently absent or abandoned. The competition is fierce and your competitor's success is often unreasonable if not incomprehensible. The challenges can seem insurmountable or certainly unsolvable. Don't despair, it is still possible to overcome all of the above and make a damn good living!

This is not meant to depress or discourage you. But to simply convince you that being insecure is the norm in both the creative and business sides of the biz. Embrace this insecurity and face your fears. Easier said than done, right?

Fear Destruction Technique. Write down a list of all your fears. Number them. Then state them out loud. Tell each fear that you will not be defeated by them. That it will not block your success. Recognizing these fears is half the battle. Otherwise, you allow their power to enhance by festering in the cobwebs of your mind. They become a dangerous obstacle to achieving your creative career goals.

Do this as often as necessary. Think of these fears as your enemies. Whenever they materialize in your thoughts or dreams, you must find a way to make them disappear, you must find a way to overcome them. Or ignore them. Like insecurities, fears are common for creative professionals. There is no set way (but dozens of books, I'm sure) to diminish or fight them, but you must try to find the one that works for you. Otherwise, these fears can snowball into a giant source of career sabotage.

"I've been absolutely terrified every moment of my life—and I've never let it keep me from doing a single thing I've wanted to do."

So exclaimed the famed artist Georgia O'Keefe. This quote is plastered on my brother's office door. He sees it everyday before he sits down to write. Celebrated artists may not speak about this in slick magazine interviews or television talk shows, but the majority of successful and acclaimed creatives certainly have had fears of their own. They have somehow discovered what to do. How to cope with them, ignore them, or wipe them out.

The creatives who succeed never let their lack of security or confidence derail their momentum. Fears and insecurities are never a reason to fail or quit. But you would be surprised at how many careers of aspiring actors, writers and other artists have been crippled by fears and insecurities. If not wiped out. This is a tragedy. Who knows how many of these talents would have succeeded if they found a way to overcome such feelings. What extraordinary films, books and paintings may have been created? Please don't let this happen to you.

As my friend Aristotle and many others have stated, the first part of solving a problem is to identify it. Once you have identified your fear, you must once again understand that possessing such a fear is completely normal, particularly if you're creative. I'm no psychologist, but allow me to declare the main culprits in no particular order:

Fear of failure
Fear of success
Fear of not being good enough
Fear of not being liked or respected
Fear of inadequate training
Fear of uncertainty
Fear of the future
Fear of people or various types of people
Fear of competition/competitors
Fear of being tested
Fear of critics, or gatekeepers, or reps
Fear of completion
Fear of fear itself (thank you FDR)
Fear of _____ Name your fear!

What fear or insecurity do you have? I've had a number of the above but have not let it stop me from pursuing my creative goals or trying to makes things happen. Understand that possessing these fears are once again common and normal. Keep on going!

Think of yourself as a medieval guard protecting a castle-- except that you are the castle. When an intruder appears, you will fight it and prevail. Your king and country depend on you to do your job. It's the same with a fear or insecurity. In this case, it is your art that needs your protection. Fight the fear with your entire personal arsenal; with all the weapons at your disposal. Any way you deem necessary. If a fear or insecurity returns for any reason, don't hesitate to take it down again. You make not kill it, but try to push it away.

Some of us have found a way to simply transform our fears or insecurities into our advantage. That's right, this is also an option. It may be just a matter of transforming self-sabotaging or negative energy into positive energy.

The world is waiting. You believe in yourself and I'll bet you're pretty damn good at your craft—or you probably would not have picked up this particular book. Let me tell you something. Lean closer so you can hear. It is your artistic and communal duty to share your gifts with the world. It's not just about you, you follow me? In other words, it's not only an ego thing--although that can be motivating for some. No, it's about your talents and your obligation to the community as well as to yourself.

As an artist, you have God-given abilities that are meant to be seen! Not dusted or thrown into a closet. Not repressed deep into the crevices of your hopes and dreams. As we have established, having insecurities or fears come with the creative territory. Besides continually diagnosing and fighting your fears, there are several other tools you should use.

Silence. In the current sea of data and technology in which most of us are barely staying afloat (if not drowning), it is incumbent upon you to take time out of your busy day to remove yourself from all text, data and media. **Your artistic time**. There is way too much noise and information in our current daily lives. The effect of all this can be extremely detrimental to a creative person. This precious **artistic time** can be used to relax, meditate and monitor your breathing. Reflection is also essential as an artist because it allows you to digest and organize your experiences, priorities and life. Most important, **artistic time** compels you to turn off when you are practicing your craft. Turn off the phone, turn off the computer, turn off the TV and any other distractions to allow yourself to perform at your best.

Visualization. This may be the most important use of your silent time. Now and then it is critical that you visualize your success. Whatever internal or external obstacles exist, think about how you will overcome them. Focus on what will happen, how you will succeed and how that success will impact your life. How does that success make you feel? Stay there for a while. Isn't this fun? Are you doing all you can to generate this creative success? Make sure to later jot down any thoughts, strategies or necessary adjustments that enter your mind. Repeat on a periodic basis.

Fake It Til You Make It. In its heyday during the economically robust 80s, ICM or International Creative Management was the largest entertainment, literary and newscasting agency in the world. As discussed in **Those Early Years Chapter**, I started there in the mailroom pushing a mail cart around and distributing letters and parcels to various assistants, most of who were clearly more connected than this frazzled Ivy League graduate. Many didn't even deem to communicate with us—this was apparently beneath them. Others would complain about the most mundane things. How the movie scripts were stacked or the effectiveness of a particular pencil eraser—as if we designed the office supplies.

After almost a year in ICM's mailroom "training program, " I was finally promoted to an assistant for a wonderful guy named Randy Chaplin. He was very generous and really taught me the ropes. Not just the tricks of the trade, but the trade. He allowed me to research and suggest new clients as well as buyers. At the time, many ICM agents were threatened by their assistants and merely utilized them as clerical support. Not Randy, who was very secure in his profession and grateful for my input. I would be allowed to listen to his telephone conversations with both clients and buyers (a tradition at entertainment agencies) and I learned how to sell and negotiate from one of the best. We achieved a smooth working relationship.

Soon, I was actually negotiating and closing a few deals of my own, subject to the approval of Randy and occasionally, his boss. Word travelled fast, however, because I learned to bond with our clients bigtime and they most probably talked me up to Randy, his colleagues and bosses.

After about nine or ten months, I walked into work and went into Randy's office to see if he wanted a coffee. The office was completely empty. The sofa, plaques and paintings on the wall, files, papers, even plants—all gone. Only the desk remained and, I'm going to date myself here, a lonely Rolodex (circular spinning file) cowering in the corner. That was it. I was astonished. There was no notification whatsoever. No cell phones at that time so there was no way to reach Randy. I went back to my cubicle and waited. I was scared—was I about to be fired?

An hour of trembling followed and suddenly a call rang out. It was Randy's boss or the President of ICM who summoned me at once. I took what I thought was a career death march into a corner office on another floor of the NY ICM office. I was told to sit down and the President told me that Randy had "defected" to our archrival, the William Morris Agency (now William Morris Endeavor). How would I be fired exactly?

"We know you're helping to sign clients, we know you've been making deals. How would you feel about taking Randy's job?" I was both gob smacked and speechless. I then launched in to Jackie Gleason's "hummina hummina hummina" speech from "The Honeymooners." This went on for an embarrassing length. Finally, I was able to slow down. I nodded heartily and mouthed "y-yes."

Unlike most entertainment agencies, most of the clients at ICM were name clients meaning they were very well known if not completely famous. They could also be very demanding as they had a right to be--they were earning huge commissions for our company.

They asked every question you could imagine about their careers, goals and their lives, for that matter. Should I do this engagement or that? Should I stay with my manager? How do I get out of this contract? Is there any way to boost my fee on this gig? What book, record, play, or film should I do next?

As I was in the process of speaking to each and every one of Randy's, uh, make that my clients over the next two weeks, I understood that I would not have all the answers. I may not have any of the answers. But it was important to sound like I knew what I was talking about. I was in a humorous bind—I was a fledgling agent who suddenly was forced to make decisions and give career advice to these famous clients. I instinctively knew I didn't have a choice: if I didn't give adequate answers, they would leave me so rapidly, it would make my head spin. I grasped what I had to do: **Fake It Til I Made It.**

Believe me, I was in a precarious situation because I hadn't really "made it" in the least. If I screwed up, I could be fired quite easily. But I had to try to answer their questions, I had to try to do this job, and I had to succeed at it. Despite giant gaps of ignorance and huge lapses of essential experience I hadn't quite earned it yet.

In those early weeks, I often had to pretend or fake it. That's right—make up answers to the best of my abilities. But what is the alternative? To give up or walk away? That was not going to happen—and given similar circumstances, you must never let this happen to you.

I was thrust into a familiar situation for anyone in the entertainment, media and art world who just got hired, promoted or financed. For anyone reaching or attaining that coveted next plateau. It is almost a rite of passage in our world. Whenever you have an opportunity to expand your horizons and experiences. Whenever you can promote or advance yourself, always but always accept the challenge. Take the leap! Even it means you must **Fake It Til You Make It.**

Jump into it without hesitating in the least. It is a standard part of our biz to learn on the job. **On the job training.** If you have the time, try to research and interview anyone who has done what you're about to do. Try to avoid giving away that you're not fully qualified by qualifying the question. Ask how is it done here? Or on this set? Or in this city or country? Get the picture?

Think about this: what is the worst that can happen? That you'll be discovered? First of all, this rarely happens. If it does, you can try to cover whatever you did in any creative way you can. There is no death penalty for faking your way into a job as far as I know.

What happened to me will most probably happen to you. After a month or so, my knowledge and expertise filled my gap. Pretense was overtaken by wisdom. That is, I learned my job. I learned the right decisions to make, the right things to say; the best advice to give. In the same way, you will learn to do your job much quicker than you think. Take the risk.

Confidence is King. The underlying theme of this entire chapter is quite simple: Confidence. With a business that is as unpredictable, insecure and unstable as ours, there is nothing as important as having confidence in yourself. You must learn to believe in yourself. How can others believe in you and your abilities if you don't? They simply will not hire or rep you if they don't have confidence in you. Too much is at stake. They want to have the confidence that you will make them look good. They want to solidly believe that you are the best person for the job, or the best possible client or the best artistic investment. They will not take the risk of working with someone who makes them feel uncertain or unsure in any way. They can't afford to hire the wrong person or potentially cripple a production, company or crew.

How do you convince them? One way is to be excited about yourself. How can you convince others to be excited about you and your abilities if you are not excited first? The best way to convey such passion is to exude confidence. If it doesn't come naturally, work hard on it. Few of us are confident 24-7-365, but we are on when meeting someone who can hire, rep or finance us (aka a **primary contact**). This is absolutely crucial.

Confidence is perhaps the most important ingredient for success as a creative professional.

Confidence is conveying the feeling that you can do the job. That the powers-that-be can rely on you whatever the circumstances. That they have made the right choice by picking you. That you will surpass their expectations. That you are the one.

Not all of us are confident forces of nature. If you happen to be an actor or actress, simply pretend to be the most confident person in the world when you're meeting someone that can impact your life. That is your new role. **If you're an actor, act!** Don't be arrogant or aloof, mind you. That is not the same as confidence and is most often viewed as obnoxious.

For those of you non-actors who have trouble with confidence, try this. Think about how talented you are, how much you want to reach the next plateau, how much you want to achieve your creative career goals, how much you deserve recognition, acclaim and applause for your talents—and allow these feelings to push you into a confident state of being for whenever you need it. Now practice repeatedly. Are you getting there? Practice again. This is not just a choice, it is a necessity.

* * *

GET IN THE GAME!!

Congratulations! You have entered or are about to enter a field where there is no formula. Nada. Nicks. Klum. Rien. Zip. Zero. Squat! Does this mean you should immediately throw in the towel? No way, Jose. But to blindly proceed down a worn path that some notables have used years or generations ago may not be practical either. Blindly following the other artistic lambs or lemmings won't do the trick. Instead, you need to distinguish yourself, specialize, stratify, schmooze, network, learn the business and find the buyers. We will delve into each and every one of these pursuits in other chapters of this book. But first, are you in the Game?

If you ask the so-called experts, each may have their own thoughts on what is the best formula. But you'll find none of them has the "answer." The answer most probably depends on you, your personality and specific talents. Some of the famous just got lucky—they were at the right place at the right time. Some may have just known the right person or someone who knew the right person. Others have absolutely no idea what their formula was. They don't really have a clue how they got to the Promised Land—they just did. But one thing is for sure, **they got in the "Game."**

In any creative career pursuit, there are those in the Game and those on the sidelines. What is the "Game?" Where do you stand? What is the difference? It's quite simple, really. In a field that altogether lacks a formula, the Game is a way to measure your progress. And how far you may have left to go. Those in the Game are the next wave of the successful. They have chosen which strata of their field they wish to operate. They have selected those buyers and reps who are best suited for their particular talents. They have also made repeated attempts to know them and get their work out there.

For the beginning or aspiring creative professional, the Game represents the achievement of the first wave of necessary short term (1-3 + years) goals. It doesn't mean that this is the end of the road. Or that nothing else needs to be done. No, it is the beginning, but being in the Game signals that you are well on your way. If you're on the sidelines, it is also crucial sign that that you may have to progress on that creative career ladder. Perhaps, you need to change or accelerate your approach. What are you doing right? What are you doing wrong? From the sidelines, you need to figure it out.

Indeed, the Game serves as a giant career marker of sorts. It tells you if you are on the right track and what you have to achieve to get there. Yes, I know it's not easy. Little worth achieving in life is easy. You probably have well publicized stories of those who have obtained fame and fortune quickly. I assure you that these are insanely rare—maybe one in a million. The usual "overnight" success is one that requires extremely hard work, devotion and ingenuity. And the ability to adapt to changes, whether economic, industrial or cultural. The Game is but one marker which is welcome in a field which full of misinformation. An industry where there are numerous articles and books on the craft but almost none on actually making a living from that creative profession.

The Game for Actors. There are three crucial requirements for getting in the game as an Actor:

a) You have joined both actor's unions: AEA (Actors' Equity Association), SAG-AFTRA (Screen Actors Guild- American Federation of Television and Radio Artists) for theater, film and television, respectively. The later union is the result of a recent merger by what once were two separate unions.

Now joining one or both of these unions may be premature if you're just starting out. It also may be ill-advised if you don't live in NY or LA because there may be a lot more non-union work than union work. However, it is a necessary future goal because it will legitimize you in the eyes of an actor's Primary Contacts: Agents, Managers, Casting Directors, Producers or Directors. That is, they will see you as the real thing, a true professional or even better--one of them.

In addition, the unions often are the first to list auditions on their actual or electronic bulletin boards. They also have professional workshops that are free or discounted. And they have meetings with other members, whom you will have the opportunity to meet. These fellow union members may have a lot more experience and contacts than you. Why is this important? Because they may be a great source of important industry knowledge and scuttlebutt: Who are the best Agents and Managers at your level? Are any Casting Directors accessible or approachable? Who are best teachers in Acting, Audition Technique, Voice? When is that audition happening? You know, the one to be directed by the brother-in-law of your new union member friend.

Beyond such info and scoops, you may be fortunate to become friends or creative partners with these members. They may then introduce you to their contacts. For example, their agents and managers (particularly if they are not a similar or competitive type) or various buyers they know. Yes, it can absolutely happen this way.

b) You have an agent or manager. You're in the game if you have one, but I believe in both. I often hear actors complain about that additional ten or fifteen percent in commission, but 15% of nothing is nothing, you know? As I've elaborated fully in the Actors & Managers Chapter, think of yourself as a political cause and your agent and manager as lobbyists. The objective is to promote that political cause as widely as you can. Why have one lobbyist when you have two? Even better when they are not in the same social or business circle. Then your cause (you and your work) can be promoted to an entirely new wave of supporters (buyers) with whom each of your reps drinks, eats, play golf or God forbid, even fools around!

You should learn the business as well as your reps does—it's not rocket science. Indeed, you also should research and learn about the buyers as well as your agent and manager. Who are buyers best suited to your particular skills and talents?

Complement your rep. Only with this knowledge will you able to effectively complement your agent and/or manager. No, I don't mean to compliment or praise them (although this always helps in our business), but to work with them and complement their efforts in getting you the next job or to the next career plateau.

c) Most of the casting directors in your city know you on a first name basis. That's right—as an actor, you need to know these people and they need to know you. You can't be a vague talent or a mysterious individual (although a bit of mystery can go a long way) to them. They should know what kind of actor you are. What is distinctive about you? What are your strengths and assets? What is your background? What have you done? Which of your friends or champions do they know? What roles or jobs are you right for?

Yes, there is mucho competition and possessiveness on the part of other actors when it comes to knowing casting directors. And understand that they may not be the most approachable human beings in the world. But don't ever let this stop you! And don't fear them--you must make this happen. **In order to make a living, you will need to find some way to meet most, if not all, of your local casting directors--and hopefully impress them.**

If you have not achieved all three of these acting requirements for the Game, do not despair. Not everyone is there yet. However, thousands of actors have done so. Let the Game serve as a short-term goal for you.

If you are planning to make a living from your acting skills, you will need to do all three of these. Don't let this depress you. Don't let this dampen your spirits. Don't let it transform you from an optimist into a pessimist. Do let it focus and galvanize your efforts. Getting in the Game is not done overnight. It may take you from three to five years. But now you simply know what needs to be done to proceed to the next level.

The Game For Other Creative Professions. If you are not an actor, please feel free to devise the right game for your craft or profession. Choose a set of accomplishments which can be achieved in three to five years, if not sooner. There should be hundreds of your fellow craftsman who have already succeeded in getting these done. They are further on the path towards making a creative living.

Although you may better served by devising a game of your own, here are several Games for Other Creative Professions examples that will hopefully guide and motivate you:

The Game for Directors
a) You have an Agent or Manager.

b) 30 Producers/Production Executives in your specific genre know you and your work.

c) 20 Distributors/Sales Agents know you and your work.

d) 10 Film Financiers know you and your work.

The Game for Writers
a) You have an Agent or Manager.

b) 30 Buyers know you and your work. Depending on whether you are a Screenwriter, Journalist or Author, these could include: Producers/Production Executives, Periodical Editors, Book Editors, Publishing Executives, Website Content Bloggers or Providers, Advertising Executives, among others.

c) You have at least three major proposals/projects.

The Game for Producers

a) You work with a respected Agent, Manager or Lawyer.

b) You know a combined 100 other Producers/Production Executives and Film Financiers.

c) 30 Distributors/Sales Agents know you and your work.

d) 20 Prominent Actors' and Directors' Agents take your calls/ meetings.

e) 20 Film Festival Heads and 20 Entertainment Journalists/ Bloggers know you.

The Game for Artists

a) 20 Art Gallery Owners/Dealers know your work.

b) 10 Artist Reps or Artist Consultants know your work.

c) 10 Museum Curators know your work.

d) 5 Art Critics know your work.

e) 30 Art Collectors know you and your work.

The Game for Musicians

a) You have a Producer, Music Lawyer, Manager, and Booking Agent.

b) 20 other Music Lawyers, Managers and Booking Agents know you and your work.

c) 5 other Producers in your musical genre know you and your work.

d) 30 Venue Directors/Bookers know you and your work

e) 10 Music Critics/Bloggers know your work.

f) 10 Recording Executives know you and your work. That is, if they still exist by the publishing date of this book.

Your Game Progress. Once you start pursuing these goals, you must ask yourself: How much Game progress am I making? Are there any impediments or obstacles in my path? What can I do to overcome them as soon as possible? You must continually gauge where you are in pursuit of your Game. Avoid self-sabotage and rationalization however tempting these habits may be. Just figure out what the Game is for your desired craft or profession. What do you need to do to get there sooner? Any adjustments you need to make?

Try to avoid belittling yourself in the process—it is a challenge but you can get it in the Game!

Future Games. If you are you in the Game, you may want to devise the next game for yourself in pursuit of greater success and name recognition in your chosen field. It is essential to establish parameters to measure your progress. As all studies indicate, if your goals are specific and monitored, they are much more likely to be achieved. What is your next Game? How long are you going to give yourself to achieve it? Are your reps on board with it? Do they have any reservations? Good luck and Godspeed.

* * *

EVERYTHING YOU ALWAYS WANTED TO KNOW ABOUT AGENTS & MANAGERS, BUT WERE AFRAID TO ASK!

There are a plethora of myths, untruths and half-lies about agents and managers also known as reps. Particularly as they relate to those of us who aren't yet stars. Hopefully, this chapter will dispel of most of these. We will also discuss the distinction between agents and managers, which, like modern-day Republicans and Conservatives, is becoming slimmer and slimmer if not negligible.

Aspiring creative professionals equate obtaining an agent or manager to winning a lottery. If only this was true. If only you were fortunate enough to obtain a rep, then everything would be easy street. You'll probably book a gig in the following week. Unfortunately, this is the view of many aspiring creatives. If only I had a rep, everything will be cool. I can chill at the beach and wait for the phone to ring. Yes, I get it--a real panacea, a real cure-all. Am I right? All of your career stumbling blocks out the window. Your road to riches and worldwide fame will now be assured. As many of us with reps know only too well, this could not be farther from the truth.

Not that you shouldn't be happy to have an agent or manager who is willing to lend their reputation to yours. They will hopefully introduce you to some people who could actually hire you now or in the future. They will hopefully teach you about the business; about which buyers are hiring—particularly those who could use and enjoy your particular talents. Many of those potential employers may be close friends of theirs. **But the reality is that most reps are only effective in the upper echelons of your career when you are already someone, when you have a name or serious reputation in your skill set section of the entertainment, media or art world.**

But this should not stop you from learning as much as you can about agents and managers—and which of them may be best for you.

Agents. Depending on the art form, their function may differ, but basically they have a lot more clients than managers. The average actor's agent probably has 50 or more clients. They take a 10% commission of your earnings. They are very specialized—screenwriting agents are a different brand of agent than book agents—although both are called literary agents. There are specific agents for clients in commercials, new media, reality TV, electronica, video games, and sports. There are agents for bands, singers, comedians, motivational speakers, costume designers, photographers, designers, line producers, costume designers and orchestral conductors.

Agents are about booking, that is, covering their expenses. At most large agencies, they have to make at least three times what they and their staff cost. The smaller the agency, the less they need to make to cover their own yearly nut (total expenses). At larger agencies, there are in-house lawyers who can take care of most of the legal paperwork needs of clients. At ICM, we also helped with insurance, travel, immigration, personal shopping and house theater or concert tickets, among other absolute necessities. :)

Agents usually have much more leverage (bullying power) than managers. If they really want to get you a small role in a small film, TV show or play, they can theoretically hold back the star unless the powers-that-be (the producer, director) take you too. Get it? That is called leverage. Agents can be more ruthless in cutting clients than managers. If you are not performing, that is making enough bucks for the agency, they may drop you within several years or less.

This elimination or filtration process used to affect only the least performing ten to twenty percent of the agency's clientele. With the recent recession, however, some agencies have been know to rid themselves of an even larger percentage of clients. Sometimes up to

50%! In addition, over a third of the lowest performing agents have been laid off (e.g. forced out or office tortured into resigning, not rehired, etc.) in the last few years. Many of the rest are fighting for their jobs in an especially ruthless, dog-eat-dog epoch of our business. So have some understanding why many agents in the middle or larger agencies are not always in the best of moods. If they ever return your call, that is.

More Agent Knowledge & Advice. The four biggest agencies are (in no particular order): CAA (Creative Artists Agency), WME (William Morris Endeavor), UTA (United Talent Agency) and ICM (my alma mater--International Creative Management). Then comes the following in no particular order: Gersh, Paradign, APA (Agency for the Performing Arts), and Innovative. After this grouping, next comes a number of middle agencies, including but not limited to: Abrams, Don Buckwald, Metropolitan, and The Gage Group. If you don't have a name or presence yet, you will probably not have a chance at any of these. And that's okay.

Because here is the big reveal of this chapter: **How well-known your agent/agency is not the right question--how much time your agent spends on your career is the only question.** The former is nice to brag about or pretense in a cocktail party. "Oh me, I'm with CAA" (along with a smug "fuck you" grin I'm guessing). But if your supposed CAA agent only spends five minutes a month on you, guess what? You have an agency in name only. Is it better than having no one? I suppose, but they are simply order takers. That is, they only answer the phone on your behalf. If you're lucky. **You want your reps to be order makers. That is, those who will call buyers on your behalf and not just wait for them to come out of the woodwork.** Capice?

It is much, much better to have a smaller or medium sized agent or even a one man operation—say Joe Snooklick for the Joe Snooklick Agency--who is spending an hour per week order making on your behalf than a big agent who is doing very little on your behalf. And you never know, Joe Snooklick may just be the next Ari Emmanuel or Jeff Berg. If he is working hard and producing results, be loyal. Don't jump to a bigger agent just because you can. Whatever their lofty pitch, chances are you will be lost and forgotten within a year or two. And it is not right. **Be loyal to those who were loyal to you. Certainly to those who pushed your career to the next plateau.**

Harrison Ford has had the same manager, the late Patricia McQueeney, for 35 years. I'm sure he received multiple offers from every major manager and he rejected every single one of them. Surely, his career was not affected by his loyalty to the manager who signed him when he was much more of a carpenter than an actor. And there are countless similar stories about staying loyal to high performing agents and managers.

Partnership. Often, the most successful and effective partnerships (between actors and agents or writers and agents or clients and managers, artists and gallery owners or actors and directors, etc.) are those where the partners rise or succeed at the same time. They rise as you do and vice versa. They succeed in, more or less, the same time frame as you. And often, at a similar pace. This is the natural order of things in the creative world.

The fantasy that a hugely powerful agent or manager (or director or editor or gallery owner, etc.) will suddenly take you (assuming you're not already a name) on and lead you to the promised land of fame and fortune is extremely rare. **Rather, you should rely on someone who is as hungry as you to succeed. Someone for whom the stakes are just as high.** This way, you'll be right smack in the bull's-eye of success probability instead of clawing onto a rusty pipe dream.

Managers. In theory, managers have much fewer clients (usually from 10-20) and can give you more individualized attention.

They usually take from ten to fifteen percent of your earnings. Twenty percent for some creative professions. Their representation can cover all aspects of your career. For example, if you're an actor, the commission would usually include all your work in commercials and voiceovers, not only films, TV and theater or your "legitimate" representation. And sometimes your writing and directing gigs to boot if these exist. In exchange, managers will give you much more of their attention than an agent. They may even attempt to obtain constructive feedback from buyers who rejected you, almost unheard of from busy agents.

Great managers will put more time into building and strategizing your career over the long run. They are also into booking as much as agents since this is how they make their dough. Most managers will be more likely to approve lesser paying jobs to further or "stretch" you career. That is, to make you more marketable in the future.

For example, they may be more willing than agents to look the other way or approve of your work in lower budget or independent films and theater. They will try to fight against how you may be pigeon-holed or stereotyped in the industry. They are more willing to take the necessary risks to build a multi-faceted and impressive career.

Managers are not supposed to negotiate on behalf of their clients. In fact, in some states like California, they are forbidden to do so. But it happens. If an acting client is wanted for a specific role, the wise agent and manager usually defer to the rep who best knows the buyer (e.g. producer, production executive, director, casting director). This may happen even if the other initiated the pursuit of the role. A good agent-manager partnership is contingent upon honest and open communication. That is, a good exchange of opinions along with a thorough discussion of the pros and cons of the various career choices. It is these choices, after all, that make a career.

Often, a successful client's schedule is limited. For example, it could be a TV star who is on hiatus for three months. The agent may want the TV star to accept a silly and brain-numbing formula studio film for the big bucks. The manager may want the client to do an edgy independent film which showcases the client's intensity and "chops" (acting prowess). Sometimes, the client may want to do neither and just chill with their family after eight months of 18-hour days. At any rate, good reps can chew on the options until the best solution is found.

Like Harrison Ford, clients are usually more loyal to their managers than agents and stay with them for a much longer duration--if not their entire careers. One of the most important functions of a manager is as an agent overlord if you will. They make sure the agent is doing their job well. They are a better gage at this than you are. This is why it is important, if possible, to try to avoid selecting agents who are close buddies with your managers and vice versa. If they are close friends, there is limited leverage (show biz bullying power) over one another. Get it? Otherwise, you have the serious leverage of potentially firing the agent or manager if they don't perform.

Agent _and_ manager? Yes, absolutely. Forget about the double or higher commissions for a moment. What is the saying? Twenty-five percent of nothing is nothing. If you're successful, it is about sharing the enormous workload that has snowballed into your very demanding and brilliant career. Whether you are an aspiring or working creative, it is about getting the word out about you.

There is yet another reason why your manager and agent should not be close friend, if possible. If they're friends, they may be from the same social groups/networks and know many of the same people. This duplicity is not helpful to you. You want your reps to be from entirely different, but no less powerful or useful, social orbits. Two separate reps who are introducing and praising you to their distinctive social networks.

Let me stretch our analogy. The (your name) campaign is much more effective if you have two separate forces lobbying in that vast entertainment world (or at least among the meaningful buyers) on your behalf. They can inform you if the other is not doing their job. You'd be surprised at how many well-known or established clients are saddled with reps who are not doing their job. Some may not even have a clue.

A Caveat. Again, I don't mean to cause a stampede away from your reps for two major reasons. One, they may doing their job well and you simply don't know or appreciate it. Or you are inexplicably ungrateful. If you are working and meeting new people in your industry, be happy. One of the reasons it can be very easy for one rep to steal another's clients is that they can promise seductive possibilities that will probably never materialize. Or the typical irrational belief that "the grass is greener on the other side of the fence." Very occasionally, it may be your lucky day, but more often than not, that grass only looks greener. Take a closer look and you'll see that the grass is merely dirt.

Eight Effective Ways To Obtain an Agent or Manager. Getting your first rep or finding a new rep is extremely difficult, particularly in a difficult economic climate. **Try to be optimistic!** Most successful people tend to be optimistic.

The following are the most effective ways I know (in no particular order):

1) They come after you. By far, the most effective technique is for your rep to read/hear/watch your work and pursue you. For example they see your acting chops in a play. Being the recipient of such a pursuit is heads and shoulders above all the other options, but usually you have to be in something (show, film, art opening, book, etc), and achieved an impressive creative accomplishment that speaks out.

Going after them is a much less effective option, but if the above doesn't happen, what choice do you have? If an agent started the process, they have much more vested in you. They want to confirm their initial instincts much like a sports coach wants to justify their handpicked selections for athletic scholarships. If they fail, you can always confront them with "Why did you pursue and sign me if you're going to do jack?"

2) A reference from a director, producer or casting director. This may carry a lot more weight than other references as these people are your reps' clients and buyers. Indeed, there could be a business cost to ignoring them.

3) A reference from a fellow agent or manager. You can't really beat this one, but make sure there is an obvious reason they cannot sign you. For example, they only work with stars. Or they are literary or commercial reps and not legitimate (film, TV and theater) agents or managers.

4) A friend or good natured acquaintance who is already a client. And guess what? They do you a favor and introduce you. This doesn't happen all that often but it can. Avoid the pursuit of those who are similar (type or category) to you (young stunning blonde actresses, dark comedic screenwriters, abstract sculptors, yet another heavy metal band, etc.). Instead ask those who are a different, if not a completely distinct type, category, age or talent. For actors, this is a reason in itself to go to an acting or audition class. For writers or artists, join that weekly meetup group now.

5) You join an organization or attend a networking event that attracts agents and managers. Seems obvious, but you'd be surprised how fearful creatives are about joining creative business groups and organizations. Or to simply spend time with those working in the business side of your craft. Hanging out with fellow actors, musicians and comedians will only take you so far. **Socializing with**

prospective reps and buyers of your talents is the answer, my friends.

6) You're in a show or event with a colleague, peer or cast mate who has a rep. The rep comes to cover a show, film or other happening and sees your talents. Voila! Obviously, you need to be in something noteworthy to begin with, but this does happen.

7) A reference from a teacher, professor or consultant. They don't like to publicize it, but yes, they know a number of reps and often work as a scout. In exchange, the reps may represent them or perform other favors.

8) A reference from an entertainment lawyer, accountant or business manager. Same as 7) above. Hard to believe, I know, but they can have serious clout. And all would have reps among their friends and colleagues. Peek into their iPhone address list now. See what I mean?

If you're a rep virgin. This includes those who may have had a rep years ago and find themselves at square one again. Don't hate or torture yourself please. It is just the nature of the business. Guess what? You're are a survivor—it would have been much, much easier to flee to the land of the civilians (non-creatives). Congratulations to all of you. But here are a few more caveats. Make sure your rep is actually doing something for you. As discussed in **Complement Them!** below, give your reps great materials, research your head off and continue to network and meet buyers on your own.

While I believe having a rep is generally better than not having one, sometimes this is not the case. Unfortunately, you may find yourself repped by that uncommon (but not rare) breed, the ever so scummy **Con Man rep.** They come in various garden varieties. They may simply be someone (could include producers, gallery owners, literary agents, film investors) who seduces you to be involved but can't deliver the goods. They may say to you that they can get you into studio films, but only know a few commercials producers. Essentially, they're pipe dreaming bullshitters and get off on pretending to be someone other than who they are.

An even more infamous variety is the manager (can also happen with entertainment lawyers) who signs hundreds and hundreds of eager clients to lopsided contracts. They pretend to be enthused by your individual talents, but really are just signing anyone they think may have even the slightest chance of succeeding.

Visualize this: they throw hundreds upon hundreds of headshots or resumes or portfolios against the wall to see which ones stick. Although the percentages may be low, basic probability dictates that a few will stick. That is, a few clients (of the hundreds) will get hired on their own (or sell their film, etc.). Without any assistance whatsoever from the Con Man rep. Then the Con Man rep man cashes in. And makes a sizable commission from you without shame and guilt. Even though they had nothing, nada, zip--to do with it.

Other Garden Rep Varieties. A less venomous variety of the above is the manager or agent that simply has way too many clients. Okay, they may actually make sales calls. They may also send their acting or writing clients out now and again to auditions, but are they vesting themselves enough into the success of a particular client? Not exactly—they just want to make the bucks without regard to anyone's career save their own. Evidence of this is meeting way too many similar (same type) clients from your agency or at the same audition.

Another particularly vexing example is one or two similar looking agency clients who are working way more than you. However, this is okay if those clients are stars or way more advanced in their careers than you are. Whatever jobs they refuse you can collect like a great wingman at a singles night out. But if you're in the same league as them, you are being dissed bigtime and should begin the process of finding another rep.

Out Clause Now! It is because of these garden rep varieties that you must be very careful before you sign a contract, letter of agreement or any other document. You must make sure your client agreement is never more than a year or two at most. **And there must be a performance-based Out Clause.** Very important!! That means you are able to get out of the contract in 3-6 months if you don't receive a paying job or don't make a minimum income (keep this threshold as high as possible like 10G after six months). If you don't have an **Out Clause,** you may find yourself paying a considerable chunk of your paycheck to a disreputable scumbag who never actively lifted a finger for you.

With agents, you are more protected. They have to abide by certain union and state franchising regulations if they are franchised/ licensed by the state (as most are required to) because they are signatories with the unions who dictate that their members may leave an agent if they haven't made any money after a relatively brief period, usually 3 months.

Agents & Managers: Vanishing Species? There are now 30-40% less agents and managers than just five years ago. And for many of these survivors, job security is an alien concept. There is simply a lot less paid work for creatives right now. Why? A combination of the following: 1) the collapse of the music and independent film sectors—the number and percentage unemployed (not to mention underemployed) creatives is unprecedented; 2) the advent of reality television; 3) the timing of the 2007 WGA (Writers Guild of America) strike; 4) the reduction in the number of studio or Hollywood films—18% fewer movies in 2010 from that of 2007— and the trend is continuing; 5) unfettered internet piracy (when will laws and enforcement come?); and 6) the particularly disgusting maldistribution of entertainment and media incomes—that is, disproportionately fewer people (than ever before) make the lion's share of the income. If you are working in a multinational corporation in any industry today, this practice may sound awfully familiar.

In other words, less creatives are earning a livable income than ever before—not that it was ever easy. As discussed, there are fewer agents and managers around. Although the big four agencies (which serve the highest earning clients) are relatively stable, the business survival of medium and small sized agencies and managers is threatened like never before. And this is not letting up, for the time being.

In addition, the competition for up-and-coming or breakout clients has become unbelievably cutthroat. Yes, there were raids in the past, but the tactics have become Machiavellian in an unprecedented way. And this is not limited to big-client signings among the top agencies. Unlike the past, bigger agencies are making their own version of drone attacks on small or mom-and-pop agencies. There was once an unwritten rule to avoid such business terrorism. To stick to poaching from agencies or companies of a similar size. Not now, I'm afraid. The bigger agencies are promising the world to hot clients whose departures could forever cripple the smaller agencies. If not ruin them.

How does this affect you? If you are an aspiring or working creative, there will be fewer and fewer reps around to service you. Those that still do business are continually shedding clients. Others have simply put a moratorium on signing new clients. Or at least those who are not already earning a certain minimum level of income. The smallest of these reps are called developmental or junior agents and you'll find their business survival is jeopardized in a difficult economy.

Complement Their Efforts! These recent developments have forced those without reps to be their own agents and managers. It has also forced those with reps to do more of their own agenting. That is, to really try to *complement* the efforts of their agents or managers. This is a good thing. **Whatever the economic climate, however successful your creative career, you need to learn to do Complement Their Efforts!** When I state *"complement,"* I don't mean lathering on praise, as in compliment with an "i", although this always helps in our world. No, I mean working with your rep as a complement; "to help, if not complete, one another's efforts" to enhance your creative career.

If you've been reading this chapter carefully, the concept that your agent or prospective agent is a cure-all is hopelessly outdated. Most successful creatives do not keep themselves in an artificial state of ignorance simply because they happen to have reps. Creatives must complement the efforts of their reps. Their required involvement in the business side of their craft is not just a recent phenomenon. A sizable percentage of successful creatives have been doing this for their entire careers. Madonna, Tom Cruise, Shirley MacLaine, Sting, Jay Z, and Ridley Scott come to mind. They are plugged in! They take an active role in the career choices they make along with their reps. They are closely involved with the strategy of their careers. They discuss and revise their goals on a periodic basis with their reps.

Even though their reps may arrange meetings for them, clients who complement never stop networking, schmoozing and meeting with those who they respect, those with whom they want to work. They never relinquish to their reps the process of meeting new people who can enhance their careers. As they succeed, they may become more and more selective, but are still open to it. These clients also realize that even the best agents and managers don't have the time or skills to do everything.

Learn and learn some more. It is imperative to continually enhance your understanding of the ever-changing business. With the astonishing breadth and diversity of the Web, this has never been more easy or convenient. Study what deals your agent/agency are making. Any innovative deals that are suited to your specific skills?

Any recent new media or Internet business applications of your talents? Any new employers or buyers on the scene? Has recent technology opened up any new doors for you?

Maybe you can widen the geographic scope of your potential income by expanding from regional to national or from national to international. **Don't rely on your reps alone to keep abreast of all of the new opportunities.**

How to Work With Your Agent/Manager: Operating Instructions. This is really important and one of the most popular questions—How do I galvanize, amp up, or, if you like, light a fire under the ass of my agent? No matter how well you're faring, you should be doing the following:

- **Meet with them face to face.** Try to do this 2-3 times a year. Phone calls, emails or texting is not a replacement! Better yet, become their friends if possible.
- **Reps pitch you.** Ask your rep to pitch you verbally? If you possess a better one-sentence pitch/rap, give it to them.
- **Improve your materials!** Ask your rep what materials or samples they send out on you. If these are outdated or deficient in any way, correct, correct, correct. If you can improve what they are sending, do it without delay. If there is something else your reps could be using, but aren't— suggest and give to them. Be sure to be selective in what materials you present because of the realistic attention constraints of your buyers (who often have child-like attention spans and a general inability to listen).
- **Your one-paragraph pitch.** Ask your rep what one-paragraph pitch (usually in emails or letters) about you are they sending out along with your materials or samples. Can it be enhanced?
- **Remember: you agent or manager is not your publicist. Unless you currently employ a publicist, you need to**

supply the best press and promotional materials you possibly can. In other words, you are your own publicist!

- **Research and Digitize.** With the advent of digital technology, is there any link, website, or reel, your rep could be sending? Is the quality of these as good as can be? If you need to do research, then do it. **If you know someone (IT specialist, techhead, web designer, editor, blogger, etc.) who may know how to do it better, now is the time to ask for their help.**

- **List of Buyers. Provide your rep with a list of all the buyers you know or have met. Provide your rep with a list of any other powerful individuals you know or have met in your industry.**

- **List of Ideal Buyers.** Do some serious research on your buyers via meeting and the Web. Provide your reps with a list of buyers that you should meet. Please be as realistic and non-delusional as you can. **Create a select list of ideal buyers who operate in your genre, budget range and could actually hire you or those with your specific skill set or talents.**

- **Analyze This.** Do an objective evaluation of the response of your reps to these requests. If they are completely unresponsive or, shall we say, less than willing, then ask them again in a month. If you encounter the same resistance, then know your tenure as their client should definitely be considered short term.

Take this to the bank. I'm not the most spiritual person in the world, but remember this: God helps those who help themselves. Add this to the famed Turkish idiom, "Don't rely on your father." **Meaning: Never solely rely or depend on others for your creative career success.**

If you have a rep, great, but it's not the 1950's. **It is incumbent upon you to work with your agents and managers as much as you**

possibly can. Be part of the marketing, publicity and strategy of your career. Supply your reps with a list of the buyers you know (or have recently met) and a list of ideal buyers, continually revised and improved reels, resumes, bios, slides, portfolios, demos, and other tools that aid your promotion and success. Make sure you are aware of the latest technologies and how they can help you. Research! If you have a rep, convey this to them. Make sure to be optimistic and keep the faith!!

* * *

LEARN THE BUSINESS! MEET THE PEOPLE!

L earn the Business. There is perhaps no greater fallacy for creatives striving to succeed than to deliberately seclude or sequester themselves from learning the business. Your excuse may be that you are creative, but this is no excuse. **Stop secluding yourself from learning the business because you are creative—it is precisely because you're creative that you need to know the business!**

Presumably, your fellow actors, writers and artists believe that the commerce of their talents should be left entirely in the domain of their agents, managers, dealers or other business representatives. Once again, this could not be further from the truth—or the reality of succeeding today. I'm sure in the 1940s and 50s such behavior could be condoned or even justified. When asked about her next film, the foreign starlet would whine while petting her mink stole "Oh, dahling, you must speak to my agent…he knows everything." Not any more. No, no no. *Hell no.*

In a day and age when agents and managers are losing their jobs like never before (some sources estimate 300 to 400 less agents than a year ago); in a time when Ari Emmanuel, head of William Morris Endeavor (and inspiration for agent Ari Gold on HBO's "Entourage") was recently quoted as wanting to focus only on the top earning five percent of their clients; when the remaining employed agents and managers are routinely ridding themselves of their least performing (as in income) 20-50% of clients, there has never been a more crucial time to **LEARN THE BUSINESS!! That's right—you should Learn the Business that compensates and represents your talents as well as your paid representatives do. I cannot stress this enough. In this case, the commission is your career!**

KNOWLEDGE IS POWER! The more you know, the more of a chance you have at success. Of course there are other factors, like talent and connections, for example, but this can certainly give your career a big boost. Please understand, we're not asking you to neglect your art or creativity in any way. But it is imperative to learn as much as you can about the business. Otherwise, the path to greater success can be much more difficult if not downright mysterious— that is, more mysterious than it already is.

No matter how shy, uncomfortable or bored the prospect of **Learning the Business** makes you, it is an essential part of succeeding. Believe me, it's not rocket science! You can easily learn the basics and hopefully a lot more. Ideally, it would be great for you to know as much about the business as your agent or producer or art dealer. If not more.

You should force yourself to understand who are the players and buyers (of your talents), the changes and trends, and every other salient part of your industry. As we know, the time to rely on an agent or manager alone has left and gone. You may be fortunate enough to obtain such a representative, but you must learn to complement their efforts. One great way to do this is to research, network and have a clear understanding of those who are most likely to hire you, purchase your art or best represent you.

Let's use our wonderful vacuum cleaner model, shall we? The one we discovered in the **Distinguishing Yourself Chapter.** If you were selling a distinctive brand of vacuum cleaners, wouldn't you know all about your brand? Why it is distinctive and superior? Wouldn't you know who your wholesale and retail buyers are? Who are the successful competitors and how are they making success happen? Wouldn't you know the basic requirements and future trends of the vacuum cleaner business? Are there any international advances or improvements? And which stores are selling the most of your brand? Other brands? The point is selling vacuum cleaners is part of a business. **So is selling your talents—you simply need to understand the business much better than you do now.**

The extraordinary British Renaissance man, Stephen Fry--actor, director, screenwriter, novelist, TV host and MC--recently objected to his country's taxpayer-sponsored television network, BBC, for creating "bland" programming and accused them of being afraid to take risks. Although he could've kept his opinion to himself, Fry felt compelled to let his fellow countrymen know what is happening. As a very successful creative, he could've easily rested on his laurels and continued making a strong and steady income. He could've solely done his art and ignored the business side. But that is not Stephen Fry.

Like many successful creative professionals in our world, Fry felt compelled to use his talents and his brain in making an artistic difference. A Cambridge graduate, Fry set out to not be solely dependent on his rep, but sought to learn the business early in his career. He progressed to producing films and television programs that he found appealing. Fry is also a firm believer in making things happen--he will not be deterred by the fickle and increasingly conservative tastes of today's entertainment gatekeepers.

MEET THE PEOPLE! It is imperative that you familiarize yourself with those who are most likely to represent or hire you. You must understand the business is becoming more and more stratified. You need to spend the necessary time researching and qualifying those who can help your career the most.

If you are a first-time director, it is probably fruitless to seek out the producer of "Avatar." Instead, focus on those producers who have experience making indie or lower budget films, particularly those who already produced the films of first-time feature directors. Better yet, locate or convince a TV or commercials producer to get into the film game. Or find a really rich person and convince them to invest in your film. By the same token, if you specialize in horror films, seek out horror producers, not those who have only made family films.

If you're a female stand-up comic looking for a manager, you should not target a manager whose entire client list work in soap operas or at the Metropolitan Opera, for that matter. Find a manager who has other comedic clients. They are much more likely to know those humans who hire funny people like yourself. Better yet, they may be drinking or golf buddies with those who fit this description. Also, don't be deterred if they have a huge client who is similar to you. They can market you to those buyers who can't afford their huge client.

In short, research and find your own sweet spot. First explore those who are most likely to hire you, represent you or finance your art form. Particularly those who have had success with your genre, style, budget range or level of experience. Those who, based on their credits or track record, are most suited to utilizing your talents. Comprende? This will pare down thousands of potential employers or reps to a manageable **Target List** of perhaps, dozens. Distill the vast industry into those who can seriously help you! Begin that research now!

Join Organizations Now! A key shortcut to **Meet the People** is to join organizations or groups. I know you may abhor groups or group efforts. I get it. I felt the same way when I was briefly rushing fraternities at Cornell University in Ithaca, New York. Several friends were trying to get me to join their fraternities, but I soon became nauseated at "Hey Jim, this is my brother, Chuck..." I wasn't sure whether I was in a fraternity or a monastery. Then I was witness to several intra-fraternity fights, scuffles and arguments. "Which one of my brothers stole my clothes?!" I soon retreated to a small group of likeminded independent individuals and our cozy communal off-campus household.

For those of you social types who love groups, wonderful! For the others, I'm urging you to join for one simple reason: the quest to finding a decent income for your creative aspiration is so difficult to achieve that it is necessary for you to continually develop new contacts, and to understand the trends of the business that support your talents. It is impossible to do this by yourself.

Again, joining groups and organizations does not have to be a full-time vocation, but it is a fast way to meet your peers, understand their career journeys and lessons--which can then be applied to yours. More important, you'll meet those who can hire or represent you. Almost all of these organizations, including the unions, also present worthwhile seminars and workshops in the art and business of what you do.

My Favorite Organizations. For actors, filmmakers and screenwriters, I recommend joining the IFP (Independent Film Project), ifp.org or Film Independent (in LA), filmindependent. org, which present The Gotham Independent Film Awards and The Independent Spirit Awards, respectively. The IFP also presents the Independent Film Week in New York, independentfilmweek.com. I also suggest Women in Film (males are allowed to join!), wif.org. For those creatives who have an interest in politics, you may enjoy The Creative Coalition, which happens to be a networking paradise, see thecreativecoalition.org.

For journalists, poets and authors, I recommend the American Society of Journalists and Authors, asja.org, which is a fine association of independent non-fiction writers. The group helps freelance writers particularly when it comes to understanding acceptable rates and how to avoid a surprising number of immoral employers—publications, publishers-- who don't mind screwing freelance writers. I also recommend: PEN, pen.org, American Society of Authors and Writers, amsaw.org, and for travel writers ("when in doubt, take that trip!"), Society of American Travel Writers, satw.org.

Once again, join the unions if it makes sense for you. They

have periodic lectures and seminars, which are usually rewarding and useful. Some of these events do not require union membership, so go to their websites and investigate.

If you don't happen to live in or near a major city, I would definitely use Facebook, LinkedIn and meetup.com to find a group of likeminded creatives near you. The group may not be as specific as you would like (e.g. filmmakers instead of screenwriters or writers instead of TV sitcom writers) but it is essential for several reasons. One, it's always great to have the support of people with similar goals--particularly when such goals may seem daunting at times. You never know, maybe you'll partner and collaborate with someone you meet in such a group.

Sometimes, the parts are greater than the whole. Combining your talents with another creative could produce a better result than possibly either of you can achieve alone. As you'll no doubt learn in the **Networking and Art of Schmoozing Chapters**, practice makes perfect. That is, you can practice the art of schmoozing and bonding with others. It's tremendous preparation for important meetings (or other bonding opportunities) in the future. Better yet, it can be really fun.

KNOW THE RESOURCES. Now that you are on the path to **Learn the Business and Meet the People**, it is time to **Know the Resources to help you do both. That is, to know the myriad of resources that now exist for you to enhance and accelerate your career.**

Many other successful creatives know the business as well as or better than their representatives. Shirley MacLaine blew me away in this regard. When I worked with her at ICM, she certainly knew the resources. But her knowledge of the business went way beyond trade magazine articles and scuttlebutt. She can speak at length about studios, production companies, distributors and the critical and commercial success of films. Indeed, she is also knowledgeable and conversant about entertainment law and legal terms, contracts and negotiation skills. Her words of advice on these topics almost always led to an improved set of circumstances. Her agents and producers would be foolish to ignore Shirley's advice. Can you afford to ignore her example?

Magazines, websites and blogs. Be as creative as you would like in discovering useful sources, but let's start with these. Actors should be aware of *Backstage*, *Ross Reports* and youtube.com, hulu.com and playbill.com. Actors, producers, directors and filmmakers should read *Variety* and/or *Hollywood Reporter* to study the latest production companies, financing sources, agencies, and managers that cater to your particular genre or skills. For a better international perspective, London–based *Screen International* or Screendaily.com is the answer. The unions (SAG-AFTRA, EQUITY, WGA, DGA, etc.) usually have monthly newsletters and websites (with billboards and news) that can be instructive.

Screenwriters should consider perusing *Script Magazine* or *Creative Screenwriting*, and the best business of screenwriting website, donedealpro.com. Although there is a small annual fee (currently $24/year), this is the most thorough listing of every script sale that is made public. There are several other fabulous and enlightening websites: finaldraft.com, wordplayer.com, johnaugust.com, and screenwritersutopia.com. And don't forget wga.com.

Playwrights and other theater professionals should peruse the weekly *Theatrical Index* for an up-to-date listing of most NY producers, Broadway, off Broadway and touring theater news. And which plays are being produced or have recently sold.

Fine artists should check out a trio of very useful, informational and inspiring websites: artbusiness.com, theabundantartist.com and finearttips.com. Musicians should investigate several music business/industry sources: billboard.com, hypebot.com and musicindustryhowto.com. There are also several websites designed to enable distribution: cdbaby.com, tunecore.com and songcastmusic. com.

Remove those cobwebs I know so well and take the time to get into it! You never know what can happen and there are many, many success stories.

Clip Files. When you read magazines, websites or blogs, make sure to be an **active reader**. That's right, try to find articles that have a direct relevance to you and your talents. **Cut them out, print them or download!**

I'm old school and actually cut out relevant articles and put them into one of several manila folders. But you don't have to— there is surely an easier method via your computer or the Web. As discussed in the **Networking** and **Networking System Chapters**: Is there a project, producer, director or actor you know or know directly or indirectly? Or simply have something in common with? These commonalities could include: the same street, hometown, home region or home state; the same camp, church, synagogue or mosque; the same junior high school, high school, trade school, college, university or grad school. The same acting, singing or art class? You get the picture?

Even if you have nothing in common with a potential rep or employer, is there someone or some company featured who has a similar taste or sensibility as you? Indeed, is there someone or some company you would like to work with (or for) in the future? Capture the appropriate article now. Print or file somewhere that you'll see again. Preferably in this century. Hey you, I mean now! If you blow it off, you may be throwing away a career or at least a gig! You never know.

Add to your Target List. Is there a comedy producer, music club owner, opera director, film director, TV executive producer or art critic who is in the same league as you creatively or thematically? In other words, is there a great probability they would dig your work? Are they in your sweet spot?? Are you genre buddies? Great, capture the article. Integrate it into your revised **Target List** and **Networking System** (which will be detailed in a subsequent chapter). Or at the very least, save it in some organized fashion.

Act and Make Contact. Soon you'll have a list of people or companies you can contact. And then you act on it. It's that easy. Okay, I'm simplifying—it's never easy. But at least you can distill down from the vast list of all buyers and agents.

When you properly stratify yourself in researching buyers and reps, you will find that the number of individuals who can actually help you and will take your phone call (without a reference) is not an overwhelming number. But you still must act! Make sure to act on this now or in the near future--or your research will be wasted. That is always the objective. Act and Make Contact!!

More Magazines, Websites and Blogs. Journalists should subscribe to MediaBistro.com and know the mastheads of all the magazines you want to write for. Which editors of newspapers/ periodicals or website content providers would appreciate your work and clips? If you specialize in Thailand or birds or even Thai birds, is there a giant in your field, whether a fellow writer or editor, who may be able to give you a boost? Don't forget, no matter how established they may be, they were helped and guided by someone, or more likely, dozens, on their career journey. **Believe me, many of their career angels were complete strangers.**

If you're a budding fiction or non-fiction author, subscribe to Publisher's Weekly to find the publishers and literary agents that cater to your passion. Often, you can find these folks simply by looking in the acknowledgements of similar books or authors. You should also be aware of www.publishersmarketplace.com, which is incredibly comprehensive.

Another technique: Go the biggest book store you can find or Amazon.com, wherever you prefer. Now go to the section which would display your future book—and simply look at similar books. Who are the publishers, editors, and agents who made such books a reality?

Speaking of books and websites, I have carefully cultivated my favorites for you later in the **Favorite Books and Websites Chapter.**

Find Your Niche. Okay, authors—although this applies to many other creative professionals—focus on those books in your subject range or those books somehow related to your future manifesto. Is your idea still plausible or are there too many similarly themed tomes in your way? Don't run out of the bookstore (or away from your computer) in a hysterical rage. No need to pull all your hair out. Go back and contemplate and appreciate how challenging success can be.

Now what? Throw all the similar books into the garbage? Write the book you always wanted to write anyway and everyone be damned? NO!

Have some patience and take a glance at all the books in your category. Write the titles down. Think. No, think harder! Is there a related or similar topic that is not covered by those books currently on the shelves? This may take a few days, weeks or even months. But soon, BINGO! Now you know what to focus on. Okay, maybe it was not exactly the precise subject you had in mind, but you came up with something better. Maybe it is a merger of two or more subjects/themes. Preferably a subject /theme that has yet to be properly addressed in book form. Whatever it is, you may have finally found your niche.

Musicians and artists. (need to research and interview to find the best directories and websites!) Musicians, start reading *Billboard*, and *Performer Magazine* and buy the directories of managers/booking agents provided by ASCAP or BMI. Who can book you within 200 miles? What are their names, phone numbers email addresses? What about a brief road trip to meet these flesh and blood humans? Maybe you can gradually start assembling a supportive team behind you or your band. Build a fantastic website for yourself. Link it to many similar websites.

Or go global: Who runs the top music websites that feature your type of music? Skype, call or write to these folks. They will certainly have ideas to bring you up the next rung of success. **Find your niche.** Find your fans. Build your audience.

Fine artists need to read *ARTnews*, *ArtForum*, and other periodicals that discuss the market and trends. These periodicals actually have an annual top collectors issue. Fine artists need to know the collectors, contemporary art curators, gallery owners, artists' reps, art consultants and art critics, especially in their own region. Find and grow your web of collectors. Who are most likely to enjoy your work?

Like musicians, fine artists need to create a superb website for their work, one that is extremely user-friendly for collectors, curators and dealers to use. Have easy-to-view photos of your work. Have ample slides to send out when requested. Create phenomenal promotional materials (including a selective array of interviews/ reviews if available) to display on your website and whenever you send out your wares. Describe what the work is about and why it is distinctive. Why is the work relevant to you and your life? To the world at large?

Directories and libraries. When I was just starting my creative career and had no idea what I wanted to do, I would research at the splendid Library of the Performing Arts in New York's Lincoln Center. This library remains a resource paradise where one can investigate (or even watch) a play, score or singer, etc. Here, I scanned a multitude of various and exclusive directories, covering actor's agents and managers, casting directors, producers, production companies, film distributors—to begin my initial job search as detailed in the first chapter of this book. These directories were hard to find otherwise and ridiculously expensive. Now this information is available in much more affordable directories and gratis from browsing the Web.

Some of my favorite directories: For filmmakers, directors, writers and other entertainment pros, the incredibly thorough *Hollywood Creative Directory*; for actors, writers and directors, the *Hollywood Representation Directory*; for producers and filmmakers, *Hollywood Distribution Directory*; and for musicians, *Hollywood Music Industry Directory*, all by the same publishing company at hcdonline.com. And no, I don't work for them.

For all performers, there is the APAP (Association of Performing Arts Presenters) *Membership Directory and Artists Roster*—the ultimate directory of all major and minor presenters (as in those who hire musicians, singers, comedians, touring theatrical shows, etc.) nationwide, see apap365.org. I would also suggest the NACA (National Assn. of Campus Activities) *Membership Directory*, at naca.org.

For playwrights and other theater professionals there is the extraordinary *Dramatists Guild Resource Directory*, which I recommend highly. It is a fabulous list of every entity that presents professional plays in the country. There is also *LORT* (League of Regional Theaters) *Member Theaters* at lort.org, and the *TCG* (Theater Communication Group) *Online Membership Directory* at tcg.org.

Seminars, Workshops and Lectures. Many of the above

entities also offer seminars, workshops and lectures which can be extremely worthwhile. In some cases, they are not to be missed. In the interest of full disclosure--I do four empowering workshops around the world: one that is the subject of this book, **BEYOND THE CRAFT: What You Need to Know to Make A Living Creatively, Making Your Projects Happen: Successful Film/TV Producing and Financing, The Art and Business of Screenwriting/ Writing and Effective Networking and Schmoozing (see www. jimjermanok.com)**. But this has not stopped me from continuing to go to other workshops to improve myself in various ways.

In such a competitive industry, you should strive to continue learning the art and the business sides of your craft, particularly from new sources of income like New Media. In addition to the seminars presented by the above reputable organizations and unions, always be on the lookout for seminars on subjects that you don't know, or those topics on which you may need a refresher--because the path to monetizing all of the creative fields is constantly evolving.

* * *

NETWORKING 101

Nothing is more important to success in the creative world than networking. Yet for many people, this prospect is horrifying. For us humans that are most creative, we can be very intense in our personal interactions with other people. We like to have meaningful exchanges about life's often perilous conditions and both the exhilarating and harrowing experiences we all share. We value authentic encounters with others and don't desire what we see as contrived excuses to exchange words. Indeed, the thought of networking is abhorrent to many because what they perceive as superficial chit-chat seems like a waste of time. Well, guess what? It doesn't have to be that way. Your networking technique can be as real and authentic as you want it to be. Genuinely being yourself is what I endorse. But please remember this: **If you do not network or don't network enough, the chances are extremely slim that you will succeed in the creative realm!**

Networking has been around for centuries, if not millennia. It was coined as "networking" in the 1980s when there was an explosion of social events throughout the country for the express purpose of making business connections and achieving mutual career goals. As President Calvin Coolidge put it so succinctly, "The business of America is business." This was taken to an exponential and global level with the advent of email and now is peaking yet again with the recent social media networking frenzy. Whatever technological trend is on the horizon, networking will always play a prominent role.

Even if you spent every day selling hardware, it would become clear how important it is to network. Which suppliers are offering hammers for less? Which stores are paying more for screwdrivers? I really don't know how long I can prolong this ridiculous analogy, but you get the picture. If you're an aspiring or even successful creative professional, networking is absolutely essential.

Let's start with basic economics. In terms of paid gigs, there is an enormous demand for an extraordinary limited supply of paid jobs. For each acting role or screenwriting assignment, there are literally hundreds of creatives competing. They may gain access to the competition through their agents or managers, but believe me, they are competing. And the decision maker, gatekeeper, or buyer is probably going to go with someone who happens to be a friend. Or someone they have met. Or a friend of a friend. The odds for a total stranger to get the gig based on their talent alone is, unfortunately, not that high.

Another reason is the inherent collaboration of casts and crews in theater, television, and film. We are all aware of the nasty reputations a number of famous creatives have and you can be sure that directors and producers desperately want to avoid them. Instead, they want to hire someone who can easily be part of their team. Someone who is referenceable; someone they can track through a friend or colleague. In their minds, a complete unknown, like a recluse who avoids networking, is a much greater risk to the fragile equilibrium of a film or TV set than someone they or their friends know. For many, the risk is simply too great to take.

As our mother Beverly always said in her pronounced Bronx accent, "It's not what you know, but who you know." This has always been true in the arts and entertainment business. It is common sense. The more buyers (of your creative labor) and their friends you know, the more of a chance you will succeed, particularly if they like you. It's essentially a numbers game.

By the time he became President, Bill Clinton held on to his adolescent address book of everyone he ever met. He jotted down anyone who made an impact on him, those who may be able to help him along the way. Indeed, he followed up with everyone who could make a difference in his career. He stayed in touch with them and didn't hesitate to call when he needed a favor. I would say the future President's networking system worked, wouldn't you? Two lessons here: **network and don't be afraid to ask for favors when you need them.**

Yes, there are always a talented few who succeed because they won "American Idol" or starred in an award-winning independent film or wrote a catchy book that Oprah couldn't stop raving about. But these are exceptionally, exceptionally rare. The odds to win one of these artistic jackpots is something like 1 in 100,000. Or more. In ICM, we called these people "lottery winners." You don't want to bet your whole life's passion on buying a lottery ticket! By your actions, you need to make a living creatively by realistic means. The average working creative knows 300 to 1500 people in their field. The successful or famous creatives know even more. But many of them started knowing no one. Not a soul. How many people in your field do you know? Start jotting down names now and add to the list by making connections!

By now, you know my film "Passionada," was released in over 100 American cities by The Samuel Goldwyn Company. It was later released in over 150 countries by Columbia Tri Star. Before this film became a reality, I had over 529 meetings in NY, LA, Boston, Toronto, London, Paris, Madrid, Berlin and other cities. I discuss this with my brother Stephen in the Special Features section of the "Passionada" DVD.

I met with investors, producers, production executives and others who represented these folks. I'm not saying your next film will become a reality only after you take 529 meetings, but like sales, it really is a numbers game. Meeting a large number of people is your best insurance that your next major project will happen. But make sure to do your due diligence. Research and qualify these meetings so you're not wasting your time. Find those who have a real capacity and interest to help you.

The essence of great networking is schmoozing, which is described in great detail in the next chapter, **The Art of Schmoozing**. Schmoozing is the mortar that cements the building blocks of your network together. It is a skill essential to the creative skills you possess and want to monetize. You must nurture this skill by practicing and practicing—as much you possibly can. Only in this way will you eventually conquer any insecurity, shyness, or other blocks to successful networking.

There is no greater commonality among my successful ICM clients and those of the other ICM agents than the ability to network well. Many had an instant recall to names and faces even though they met hundreds every week. Others were constantly writing down notes. And there were those who had social assistants who basically networked and followed up for their bosses. It doesn't matter how you do it as long as you do it well! Develop your own techniques and strategies. Whatever works for your personality, lifestyle, and schedule. But you must find the time to fit it into your life!!!

I was once invited to the 40th birthday party of the acclaimed author Jay McInerney, writer of the classic New York novel "Bright Lights, Big City." Jay understood the value of intensive networking early in his life. In college at Syracuse University, he was a protégé and friend to Raymond Carver. At the party were a slew of his prominent friends like the late writer-director Nora Ephron and her better half, author Nick Pileggi ("Wise Guys"), film director Griffin Dunne, socialite Carolyn Roehm…and that was just my table.

But this wasn't enough. Jay invited my close friend, famed restaurant critic and food author, Bryan Miller, because Jay decided he wanted to begin writing wine criticism. He barely knew Bryan, but needed an advisor for his latest ambition. So he appealed to Bryan on a social level, which can frequently be much more effective than keeping things on a formal level. Even though Jay achieved a high level of success, he didn't stop networking. Chances are good that even if you hit the bigtime, you won't stop using this lifelong skill.

Spread That Net Wide! Let's start with the people who make worthy networking targets from that vast population you have known. **Primary Contacts** or agents, managers and those people who can hire or represent you are the most helpful. Others who know such people or **Secondary Contacts** are the next desired category of contacts. Both are incredibly important for you to pursue. Meeting and hopefully bonding with such people can save you years!

Your Social History. Think hard about your history. Everyone you came across during some stage of your life. Who from your social world can help you get to the next plateau? They could be in public relations, advertising, or other related and tangential fields.

Who do you know? From your hometown, home region, neighborhood, elementary school, junior high school, high school, junior college, college or university, graduate school, church, mosque or temple? A friend, a friend's friend, cousin, cousin of cousin, neighbor, neighbor of neighbor, current boyfriend, girlfriend, spouse, ex-spouse, ex-boyfriend, ex-girlfriend, ex-lover—no one can be untouchable. Or too embarrassing or awkward to re-approach. Remember, your goal of making a living creatively is extremely challenging. Rack your brain. Speak to family and friends and come up with a list of all those people who are worthy networking targets.

Don't Save Contacts—They Don't Accumulate Interest! One of the biggest mistakes creatives can make is to save important or powerful contacts like they were 401Ks gathering interest in a bank. This is self-sabotage at its worst. There are numerous reasons for this behavior. If these people are friends or even acquaintances, you may not want to give away the fact that you need a favor. You might want to maintain your image as fellow successful person. You can't believe how many fall into this category.

With the present economic climate, so many of us are pretending to be just fine, thank you, when we should be asking for help! Or maybe you simply don't want to bother your successful contacts until you are much more successful yourself. Or until there are much higher stakes, a bigger deal involved. This is lunacy.

As famed radio host Barry Farber use to drive into me when I toiled for his radio show, "Don't bother the Secretary of Agriculture for a problem with your peanut butter."

Okay, let's not go crazy. While you should avoid bothering high-level people for trivial matters, you need to meet and circulate with them occasionally. Let them know about your creative goals. Update them on what you're doing and tell them that you could use their help. Can they hire or represent you now? If not, whom can they refer you to?

Learn How To Ask For Favors! This brings us to another important foundation for effective networking. **As a creative professional, you must continually bolster your feelings of entitlement and confidence.** Without this, it is very difficult to convince others to become excited about you and your career. Remember, you're persuading them to help you. One common self-sabotaging stumbling block is not asking for favors from those who can grant them. Ask, baby, ask!!! What do you have to lose? They can only say no (get used to this because a thick skin is a prerequisite) or tell you to contact them at a later date.

You should try to overcome the odds and service your talent. In fact, you owe it to your talent to get out there anyway possible and do whatever you can to ensure your success. And you better believe you deserve it. Ponder this for a moment. If indeed you are talented, which I hope to God is true, then surely this is why you're trying to make a living at it. Therefore, you are, in fact, doing a favor for anyone you ask a favor of. The benefits are mutual. A two-way street. Should they take action that leads to a gig for you, they will also look good. It will also benefit them. Why do you think Clive Davis helped bring Alicia Keys to prominence? So be bold and ask for what you need now!

Join! Join! Join! The next step is to focus on meeting completely new people. As discussed in the previous chapter, try to join as many groups and organizations as you can bear. But when deciding which groups to join, I would strongly urge you to **think outside the box**. In other words, don't just join those groups that are an obvious way to describe you, but those related or tangential groups that attract members who may be crucial for you to network with. For example, many filmmakers belong to the IFP, but this would also be an ideal group for clever actors because they could meet dozens upon dozens of directors and producers who could hire them.

The Old College Spirit. Then there is the ample opportunity presented by your college or university alma mater. Most colleges and universities have alumni reunions and get-togethers in major cities. You may even run into a classmate or friend. Almost all academic institutions also publish an alumni directory. This is a tremendous investment for you. Don't delay—buy this Magna Carta! Once you receive it, take a highlighter and star those who are in the entertainment, arts and media fields. Anyone who could potentially help you.

For example, if you're an actor, writer or director, an executive in advertising, public relations, or even the recording industry can help you get to the next plateau. They may or may not be able to find you work in their specific domains but it doesn't hurt to ask. Maybe they're not film, TV, or theater hotshots, but they have friends and acquaintances in those worlds. These **Secondary Contacts** are a mere business card away.

If you are an artist, take your alumni directory and star gallery owners, reps, art critics and the like. If you're an actor, circle directors, producers, production executives, casting directors, agents, and mangers. If you're a musician, highlight booking agents, club owners, managers, producers, and label executives. Get the picture?

Social Media Opportunities. We will delve into this deeper in other chapters, but at a minimum, you must immediately join and become familiar with Linkedin.com, Facebook, Twitter and Google+. You may also want to check out Pinterest, Instagram, Digg, Delicious, Stumble Upon, Reddit and any other websites that are popular as you read this. **Social Media Action.** In a nutshell, there are three things you must then do. Find all your contacts and add them to each of your social media sites. Each site can do this automatically via your primary and secondary emails. Join all relevant occupational groups within each website--they can be rather specific, if not esoteric. And then pursue, contact, and communicate with those members who can aid in getting you to the next plateau of your career. Spend enough time on each site to follow through with all your current contacts while continually mining for others.

Informational Interviews. One of the best kept secrets of the entertainment industry or any other industry is the ability to meet anyone you want no matter how successful or powerful. At least most of the time. Seriously. It may help to be starting out, but you don't need to be in your early twenties. Indeed, you can do this at any age or stage of your career. It's quite amazing how few people are willing to take advantage of informational interviews.

I first learned this on my initial entertainment industry 9 to 5 job search detailed in the first chapter. Prior to this, I had a few acting/stand-up comedy jobs and worked on crew for features, commercials, industrials, and music videos. In those days, long before the Web, I collected a number of exclusive directories at the Library of Performing Arts. As you know, I ended up visiting Midtown entertainment agencies, managers, casting directors, film, TV, theater and commercial production companies, producers, and directors. During the process, I met (spontaneously, for the most part) a huge number of high-level entertainment entrepreneurs and executives because I appealed to their egos. With today's post-9/11 security, this job searching/networking technique may be anachronistic, but meeting those who can help via informational interviews is still alive and well. Many of those employers I met saw a bit of themselves in me. They remembered how grueling it was when they first started--when they were probably the recipients of wise advice or great references that landed their first jobs. More about this phenomenon in the upcoming **Joy of Informational Interviews Chapter**.

Stratify, Stratify, Stratify. As I referenced previously, you must learn to **stratify your contacts**. You will encounter a number of contacts that you will have to save for the next stage in your career. For me as a filmmaker, I continue to meet primary contacts who will work with me when I have reached the next plateau of my career. In other words, there are investors/producers who only work with directors who have directed one or two films already. They will not work with first time or unproven feature directors. Do I forget about them? Do I let them fall between the cracks? Do I rip up their card in front of them? No, these are all self-sabotaging tendencies. Try to bond and even become their friend. Stay in touch with them because you never know if they'll eventually be the producer (or contact) you've always dreamed about.

Sizing Them Up. You must really try to bond with those you're meeting, particularly if you admire them. The more you bond and the more they like you, the more they will help you. You can get this intense bonding started by walking into their office (the most common meeting location) and immediately **Sizing Them Up**.

Say you are meeting a male contact, for argument's sake. Is he single or a family man? Who are in those photos near his desk? Where is he from? Which university did he graduate from? What information does the framed diploma display? Did he go to graduate school? Is his desk neat and orderly or messy and disorganized? What is his personality type? Is he quiet or outgoing? Is he suspicious or inviting? Only in this way will you be clear how to proceed.

Guess what? You are a salesperson, believe it or not. You are selling and promoting your creative labor. And like any salesperson, you must gather all the information you can nonverbally and verbally. The more information, the better. This will open a number of conversational topics which you can jump right into. This will also modify how you act to achieve the best results possible. Within limits, of course. Never stop being yourself and authentic. Focus and get into it! Bond, baby, bond!

Breaking the Roles. One more thing—the best bonding is done when you are able to break the roles. Instead of being the needy applicant and allowing the person across the desk from you to be the mighty provider or employer, try to break your present roles. If you do this, the potential for them helping you is enormous. This is not always possible. Some people who have power over you like to savor it and lord over you. But take the chance if you feel it. Be open, vulnerable, and likable. Sometimes the conversation can be much more powerful and actually transcend your respective roles at the time. If this happens, you may not only end up with a mentor, but a good friend.

Networking System: Basic Operating Instructions. As we know, Networking is crucial to your career success. Thus, it is incumbent on you to have an organized and simple Networking System. One you can call you own. A system that is easy for you to use on a daily basis. You can create this on your computer or Smartphone. I'm a bit old-fashioned and prefer your basic high school notebook with categorical dividers. Make sure you have ten or more dividers or sections. Each divider should be labeled by a specific occupation or occupational category. Those occupational categories you need to meet to progress in your creative livelihood. These occupations will include both Primary and Secondary Contacts. **Primary Contacts** will be in **bold**.

I have listed a number of sample occupational dividers for various creative careers below. These lists are by no means final. Please feel free to add or remove category suggestions as you see fit.

Actor

Agents
Managers
Casting Directors
Directors
Producers/Production Executives
Theater Directors/Producers—Local
Theater Directors/Producers—National
Well-Known Actors
Commercials Directors/Producers
Industrials Directors/Producers
Writers
Acting/Voice Teachers
Miscellaneous (Yoga/Wellness Teachers, Trainers, Union Leaders, Different Country--if you work in another country, Make-Up/Hair People, Web Designers, etc.)

Writer

Literary Agents
Literary Managers
Film/TV Directors
Film Producers/Production Executives—Local
Film Producers/Production Executives--National
Film Development Executives

TV Producers/Network Production Executives—Local
TV Producers/Network Production Executives--National
TV Development Executives
Theater Directors/Producers—Local
Theater Directors/Producers—National
Well-Known Actors
Well-Known Writers
Teachers
Miscellaneous (Novelists, Union Leaders, Actors' Agents and Managers, Advertising and Public Relations Executives, Film Festival Heads, Writing Professors, Writer's Retreat Directors, etc.)

Director

Literary Agents
Literary Managers
Film Producers/Production Executives—Local
Film Producers/Production Executives--National
Film Development Executives
TV Producers/Network Production Executives—Local
TV Producers/Network Production Executives—National
TV Development Executives
Distribution Executives/Sales Agents
Key Crew People
Theater Producers—Local
Theater Producers—National
Well-Known Directors
Well-Known Actors
Well-Known Writers
Teachers
Miscellaneous (Novelists, Union Executives, Actors' Agents and Managers, Advertising and Public Relations Executives, Brand Managers, Exhibition Executives, Web Designers, etc.)

Producer

Investors/Angels
Actors' Agents

Actors' Managers
Literary Agents
Literary Managers
Writers
Film Producers/Production Executives—Local
Film Producers/Production Executives—National
Film Distribution Executives/Sales Agents
TV Producers/Network Production Executives—Local
TV Producers/Network Production Executives--National
Key Crew People
Theater Producers—Local
Theater Producers—National
Well Known Directors
Well Known Actors
Miscellaneous (Novelists, State and International Film Commissioners, Union Leaders, Film Festival Heads, Entertainment Journalists, Entertainment Bloggers, Exhibition Executives, Web Designers, etc.)

Artist

Past Collectors
Potential Collectors
Art Collectors' Consultants
Gallery Owners—Local
Gallery Owners---National
Gallery Owners—International
Artist Representatives
Curators/Museum Executives
Fine Arts Journalists/Critics
Fine Arts Bloggers
Foundation Directors
Artist Retreats Executives
Teachers
Advertising/Public Relations Executives
Miscellaneous (Art Suppliers, Sponsor Executives, Art Professors, Arts Festival Heads etc.)

Musician

Managers
Producers
Recording Industry Executives
Booking Agents---National
Booking Agents—International
Songwriters
Union Executives
Club Owners—Local
Club Owners—National
Club Owners—International
Advertising/Public Relations Executives
Music Journalists/Critics
Music Bloggers/Fan Webmasters
Miscellaneous   (Well-Known   Musicians/Bands,   Recording
Engineers, Backup Musicians, Web Designers, Web Company Executives,
Film/TV Music Supervisors, etc.)

Networking System: Operating Instructions II. Now it is
time to create your own personalized occupational dividers. If you are
a hyphenate and have more than one career goal, then you will have
even more dividers than the examples above. If you are bi-coastal, as
in NY and LA, then you should have dividers for each coast. If you
operate in more than one country, then you should have dividers for
each country. If you have numerous web connections, think about
adding new web occupational dividers of your own design.

If you are a director who doesn't do theater, then don't use
theatrical dividers. If you are a director or producer who know dozens
of other producers, then you may not be happy having dividers which
combine both producers (as in sole entrepreneurs) and production
executives (or those who are running production companies). If you
operate in the independent film world and the studio film world,
you may want to further sub-divide your dividers to reflect both
independent and studio professionals.

If you already know hundreds of connections, you may need additional occupational dividers. If you know very few connections, don't despair—you are on the way and can now see where you need to go. Make sure you have enough dividers, within which are the future "home pages" of all the contacts you'll meet. Be positive and optimistic. And network your ass off!!

Networking System Present Contacts. Now that you've thought about this and are satisfied with your own personalized occupational dividers, it is time to proceed. For each occupational divider, I create a page for every individual I meet or already know. I write their name, phone number and email. Of course, all of these are people who can enhance my career. This should include all the relevant contacts in your social orbit, whether it be family, spouse, friends, lovers, acquaintances, etc.

Potential Contacts. Those who you have heard about, but have yet to meet. For example, if your acting classmate keeps on raving about her manager, or if your neighbor knows this producer, write the potential contact's name and details on the top of the page. Then write your contact's name in parentheses. Now this potential contact will not fall between the cracks.

In the same way, you can write down every Primary Contact name that is spit out by the Secondary Contacts you meet. Remember to put the Secondary Contact names in parentheses. Now you have a home for every contact they mention. Do the necessary research and list their contact details and add any other info you wish to include. Everything is now set for whenever your contacts introduce you to new contacts. Ask them and make it happen soon. Got it? Let's move on.

Networking System Shorthand. Let's say you're a writer and you meet a big literary agent at a New Year's Day party. You have connected and exchanged business cards. Now you write this person's name and contact details on their own page in the literary agent divider. The next day or January 2nd, you call this literary agent, who we'll call Larry. You then leave a message. Here is a **suggested shorthand guide** to keep track of these attempts, which is important. If you leave a message, simply denote this on the page along with the date as in **1/2—lm**. I actually delineate between leaving a message with their assistant or **lm** and leaving word on their answering service or **lw**. If I speak to them, but they're too busy and promise to call me back later, I will denote **½--wcb as in will call back**.

If I'm fortunate enough to actually speak to them, I write **1/2--sp**. Now, it gets really important. **You must take notes on your conversation. Did your contact mention any other names? Make a page for these potential contacts in the appropriate divider. Did your contact mention auditions, writing contests, film festivals or some piece of information that can be useful to you? Write it down!** And take action soon. I have gotten jobs this way. So can you! This new information may give you that competitive edge that takes you to the next level!

Cross Reference with Your Daybook! Make sure you own a separate daybook, or datebook, iPhone calendar, or scheduler or whatever you want to call it. Now, let's suppose that your contact either wants you to call in two weeks or two months. They're too busy or may not want to deal with you now for whatever reason. They may want to arrange a conversation or meeting for a later date. Or they may want you to come to an event at a later date. Where do you put this vital information? Don't allow these precious details to fall between the cracks! OMG! It's vanishing into oblivion.

When it comes to potential or definite dates (and times) in the future, make sure to immediately record such information into your datebook or computer calendar. Always but always, cross reference your wonderful new networking system with that of your schedule. This way, you will be prompted to make that call or attend that meeting or event. As we have discussed, persistence is everything! You may have to call this contact five times, but on the sixth, they'll see you again and may give you a gig. Now, there are only two teeny tiny ways you can sabotage yourself—by ignoring your datebook or not looking at it often enough. Don't allow either to happen!

Make the Time. Many creatives transform their entire lives into networking excursions. There is no time left for them to live an authentic life or be creative. I'm not asking you to do this. **Others spend multiple hours each day to apply their networking system, to organize, call and meet people. Whether you spend an hour a week or an hour a day, you need to make the time!** It is that important! Or you probably won't make a living creatively. It's that simple. So find a way to put networking into your routine. Learn how to incorporate it into your schedule. Make a weekly appointment for networking if you have to. If it's not a part of your life already, make it part of your life. Just start doing it or doing more of it!

Luck is when preparation meets opportunity. An organized and personalized **Networking System** will lead to many, many more opportunities than you can imagine. You simply have to take the time to use it and update. Make those calls!!

* * *

DIVORCE YOURSELF (IF NECESSARY)

Over the past quarter century, I have witnessed Steve Martin at a host of exclusive film premieres and art openings. Like many comedians, he is extremely quiet and withdrawn in public. Very rarely have I seen him engaging or passionate in his speech or delivery at these events. At best, you can expect brief yet polite answers. A minimum of conversation, if at all. However, when Steve Martin is on stage, or when he is pitching high-powered film producers, agents or managers, he is full of energy and animation. Not to mention, insanely funny. It is an amazing transformation and perhaps the main reason why he is so successful.

It is a well established reality that many of us artists and creative professionals are shy or withdrawn. I'm not a psychologist, so I'm not sure why this is true, but it is. There have been numerous studies supporting this reality. It just so happens that the skills of those who are best at using their imaginations or being creative often are inversely proportional to their business skills or their interest in doing business. Maybe it's a left brain/right brain thing. Or maybe it's just part of being human—that all of us can't be great at everything in life no matter how much we try or pretend to be.

We creatives may find the entire process of promoting oneself or one's work completely repugnant. We may find the process of networking or meeting strangers to further our creative careers something to be avoided at all costs. We may find the merger of business and art rather uncomfortable. Most of us artists are truth seekers. We may be suspicious that the selling of ourselves or our work is patently false. Or that it runs contrary to expressing ourselves in an honest and authentic way.

It is not up to me to judge whether these feelings are valid or avoidant. But I know about the intense competition and various obstacles out there and one thing is absolutely certain—**you must use all the weapons at your disposal if you want to have the best chance at making a living creatively**. Forgive me for sounding militaristic, but when an army is at war, they will use every weapon at their disposal they can to win, whether it be tanks, missiles, personnel or machine guns. In the same way, you must use all your strengths and assets to win the war of making yourself a creative professional. But make no mistake, it is a war in the sense that it is a very challenging pursuit.

It makes no sense to not use all your talents, abilities and resources to make things happen for yourself. You wouldn't drop your legs and stop kicking in a swimming race, would you? Or not use your arms in a running race? Or cover your eyes while shooting hoops? Or use a racket without strings in a tennis match. You need to use all the assets you can!

So why hold yourself back in the quest for success? The only logical reason is not because you may find the process challenging or personally repugnant, but that you somehow believe you can make it without networking or actively marketing yourself and your work. And, unless you are the lucky one of 10,000 or 100,000, **chances are you will not succeed without getting out there in a social way. Let that sink in—it just won't happen.** You need to combine your talents and work with the pursuit of those who can hire or represent you. This will never stop. As you become more and more successful, you may have to meet fewer and fewer people, but the need to meet new people will never cease.

So for those of you who refuse to learn business skills, hate marketing or networking, hate socializing with or calling strangers; for those who hate talking about your work; and most importantly, for those of you who are shy, withdrawn or private, please, please digest this: **YOU MUST DIVORCE YOURSELF PERSONALLY FROM YOURSELF PROFESSIONALLY.**

Whoever you are and however you behave socially is your own business. How close you are to your family and to your friends is your domain. How many friends you have and how often you see them is entirely up to you. You can stay in a windowless room and read 24-7 if that's your thing. **But if you want to realistically have a chance to succeed as a creative professional, you need to stop cocooning and transform yourself into a social butterfly to succeed. Particularly in the right circumstances.**

For the sake of those who need it, I'll be as gentle as I can—this is not a death sentence! It is simply an instructive warning that you need to meet a number of new people in the business side of your creative career pursuit. Namely those who can represent you and hire you. Or those who know such people. I call it networking, you can call what you will. As I'll warn you again and again in this primer, you don't need to network every hour of every day. You can start off slowly and gradually. But you need to do it as much as you can stand! You need to start making it a weekly, if not daily, habit.

If it wasn't absolutely necessary, this chapter wouldn't exist, I assure you. But there is an undeniable distinction between those creatives who network and those who don't. And guess what? Those who network are exponentially more likely to succeed.

For those of you who are actors and actresses and feel uncomfortable in your new networking roles, then do the obvious and simply ACT. That's right, just play the role of a bonding and charismatic soul who is effective at bonding with people. One who puts in the required social efforts and hopefully reaches their career goals. For everyone else, you can also act or at least pretend that you have the drive, confidence, and security to meet those who could potentially help you succeed. Or those who know the people who can help you succeed. Understand this necessity and **try to be social and network!** As much as you possibly can. The more you do this, the more positive results you will achieve. I promise. Try this for a month and you'll see.

The alternative to being social and trying to make a living creatively is to be passive. To rely on others whether they be representatives like agents and managers or various gatekeepers: production executives, producers, casting directors, artistic theater directors, art gallery owners, and music club owners. Let them find you and hire you. This may happen, but you will stand on a long line behind other creatives who are insanely connected. If you are proactive and network at a steady rate, you can overcome the, let's face it, rather bleak odds and make things happen for yourself and your career.

* * *

THE ART OF SCHMOOZING

I recently directed several comedy shorts that can be found on the internet under the heading, "Interviews Gone Wrong." One of the films starred the veteran actor, Doug Stender, a presence on the New York theater scene for over three decades. Every take I shot of Doug was a pleasure. When I gave him direction, he took it extremely well and made the slight adjustment. He was absolutely perfect.

When I finished shooting, my co-director and brother Stephen asked me, "Why is this guy not a star? Like John Lithgow or John Cleese?" both of whom he resembles. There is only one compelling answer: Doug Stender is not fond of networking. Sure he has the personality and skills. He's jovial, conversational, and friendly. But he doesn't like socializing just to further his career. Believe me, I can empathize with his reluctance, but I urge you to understand the cost of such a stance.

When I first started working at ICM (International Creative Management), then the largest entertainment, literary and newscasting agency in the world, I was delighted to meet scores of extremely successful actors, writers, directors, singers, and comedians, among other creative professionals. These notable culture creators and history makers already have much in common as I have discussed in this book, but I soon detected a vast distinction among them. Some were extremely talented and others were, sorry to say, not that talented. That's right. For the supremely talented, it is quite understandable that the crème de la crème rose to the top. As they should. It was indeed reassuring to see that their status in the arts and entertainment world was deserved and warranted. But for the others? What were they doing here?! How did they get here? How did they obtain this level of success?

I was initially stunned by this reality. Especially when I thought about all those supremely talented actors in New York who never made it to the next level. So I decided to analyze this particular breed of ICM client. How did these people rise to the top without having the requisite talent? What was their secret ingredient? There is one simple answer. They were exceptional at Schmoozing.

Schmoozing is the essence of networking. The absolute building blocks. According to Webster's Dictionary, the verb schmooze is derived from the Yiddish word shmusen, a form of fellow Yiddish word schmues or talk, which itself is derived from the Hebrew word shemuoth or news. It means "to converse informally or to chat in a friendly and persuasive manner especially to gain favor, business or connections."

As Gertrude Stein once uttered, "A rose is a rose is a rose." But a schmoozer is not a schmoozer. There are schmoozers and there are schmoozers. The run of the mill schmoozers meet as many people as they can and blurt out their rap in a fast, monotonous way. They have limited listening skills and do not make full potential of their human exchanges. They collect business cards from every Tom, Dick, and Harry and go on their merry way. They may follow up; they may not. But they certainly haven't made an impression.

On the other hand, the Olympic-caliber schmoozers are unbelievably effective, having authentic and meaningful encounters with people. Always remember that the arts profession is one of give and take. You might need that gallery owner to represent you and advance your career, but he also needs that one hot installation artist to help expand his portfolio of artists. The best *schmoozers* make a lasting impression on people who remember them days or weeks later when they are contacted again. These *schmoozers* have a tremendous advantage over your common networkers. That is, they are skilled in the art of schmoozing.

Before I delve into the art of schmoozing, I want to address those of you who may be nauseated or petrified by the thought of accosting strangers—and then bonding with them. Please be comforted by the reality that you are not alone. As discussed in the last chapter, a sizeable chunk of creative folks tend to be introverted or shy. Or simply uninterested in connecting with people in what they perceive to be a superficial, vacuous, or chit-chatty manner. They just want to focus on their career and spend their time with friends and family. I get it. Of course, this is your prerogative. But you may be depriving yourself of the opportunity of making a living creatively.

I once escorted my client, Helen Hayes, the wonderful actress and "First Lady of American Theater," into the Plaza Hotel for a film premiere. Ms. Hayes would've preferred to stay at her comfy Westchester estate in suburban Nyack, New York. As the then nonagenarian walked in, she braced herself. Then she smiled, held my arm and I heard her declare: "No question, this schmoozing has to be done."

With our changing economy, the shrinking creative world is increasingly competitive and chances are you simply won't make your creative career happen unless you schmooze once in a while. You owe it to your talent to at least try. And to do it well.

Working the Room. You should be aware that when you go to various gatherings, you will need to learn to work the room in meeting and connecting with those fine folks who can help your artistic career. As a young agent for a major agency, I had to learn this skill quickly, as you can imagine. But almost every creative name or star you've ever heard of has acquired this same ability.

In addition to using the schmoozing skills which are outlined in this chapter, speed is a definite factor in successfully **Working the Room**. There may be a finite length of time for the event or certainly a limited period that those worthy of schmoozing will be accessible.

It is thus incumbent on you to bond quickly.

Be memorable and let the conversation flow. Let them know that you would love to "be in touch" and try to exchange contact details. If they don't have a card, write down their information or input into your smartphone. Seems simple, but you would be surprised at how many important potential contacts fall between the cracks because one is not bold or quick enough to ask for their details. Or a basic lack of preparation: your smartphone battery is dead or you can't for the life of you find a pen. Don't let this happen to you.

Excuse me! Another important factor in working the room success is the ability to politely excuse yourself. So many creatives are terrified of ending conversations. Even after bonding and exchanging details. This is absolutely imperative. **The goal here is to accumulate as many high quality contacts as possible during the finite duration of the event.**

A room full of **Primary Contacts** is generally a rare happening wherever you happen to live. If someone, particularly someone (e.g. friend who does not want to be alone, aspiring creative with verbal diarrhea, has-been blowhard, smooth talking bullshitter, etc.) who is not a Primary Contact, is cornering you or monopolizing your time, you need to escape! Excuse yourself at once! Tell him or her that you need to grab a drink, make a call, go to the restroom—or, if all else fails, "Great to meet you—I'm going to mingle" should do the trick. **Otherwise, you're in danger of completely missing that brief window where you can meet, bond with and accumulate those new Primary Contacts--who may spell the difference in your creative career.**

Over Networking. Try to network in moderation. Don't go overboard, whatever you do. As I mentioned before, there are those I know in LA, New York, or London who have transformed their lives into endless and continuous networking excursions. That's right, they are available to network 24-7 365 days a year! What an extraordinary waste of precious life! After all, living well and authentically is the ultimate companion to your art. If you're spending your whole life pitching yourself, how on Earth can you create your body of work? I'm simply saying you need to schmooze to succeed, but live your life!

Schmooze like a pro. The better schmoozer you become, the more of a chance you have to reach the next plateau of your creative career. As discussed, most of your favorite celebrities happen to be superb schmoozers, particularly when they were trying to make it. The fabricated press releases, magazine articles, autobiographies, and polished talk show chats may attempt to gloss over their early years, but I promise you this truth: Almost all of them used their schmoozing skills to get started and continue to use them throughout their careers.

Others allow their confederates—agents, managers, and publicists—to do much of their schmoozing for them, while they revert back to their private lives. The most extreme hide behind a coterie of family and close friends and have little interest in meeting new people altogether. They feel they simply don't need to do it anymore as they are satisfied with their careers and their social lives. This is their prerogative.

Effective Schmoozing. For those of you who are neither insanely successful nor antisocial, let's dive in, shall we? The first quality to make you an effective schmoozer is **likeability**. Seems simple, doesn't it? The ability to be liked. But some of us are so intent on achieving our goals that we become desensitized or oblivious to how others perceive us. We may try too hard to impress others with our looks, competence or intellect. Am I hot or what? Do you know how great I am at what I do? Do you get how smart I am? We may talk too fast or too much about ourselves. We may have irritating or obnoxious habits. Our personal hygiene may be lax (think body odor or breath for a start). We may fail to actively listen. In other words, we may piss people off and have no idea why.

At this juncture, please take an honest look at how you come across. How do people perceive or take you? Is their perspective the same as yours? Exactly how does it differ? Analyze and figure this out now and you will overcome what may be your biggest obstacle: yourself.

In my career, I have had the opportunity to meet a large number of successful actors and converse with them. One night in Wilmington, Delaware, my former client Dudley Moore spent four hours having dinner with a friend and me before a performance. He had the same irresistible charm that he infused into his famed role of "Arthur." He was always making self-deprecating jokes and praising the work of those actors, directors, and conductors with whom he collaborated. He could not be more **likable**.

I recall that Dudley actively listened and asked questions about our lives. He didn't pretend to do this, but was sincerely and genuinely engaged. He was open and vulnerable and "living in the moment." He was also secure enough to laugh at our jokes far more often than he made them.

One day after work as an ICM Agent, I exited our building lobby revolving door and ran smack into Michael Douglas, who was at the peak of his stardom right after winning an Academy Award for "Wall Street." Michael's famous dad, Kirk Douglas, grew up in the upstate New York city of Amsterdam near my hometown of Schenectady, New York. It turned out that I actually knew his sweet Aunt Dottie, who worked at our local grocery store, Loblaw's.

For fifteen minutes, Michael spoke to me about Aunt Dottie, his dad, and our hometown region: upstate New York. He was immensely kind and friendly, as if we were best friends or cousins. He defined the word charming. Michael focused on me as if I was the only person in the world. He was fully engaged with our conversation and didn't meander on selfish or irrelevant tangents. Nor did he interrupt me even once. The conversation was so intense and flowing that we didn't realize a giant crowd of his admirers had formed around us. As we parted, a circle of more than sixty onlookers slowly dispersed.

I could cite similar examples for other famous artists, writers, directors, comedians, and musicians with whom I had the pleasure of meeting. Those people who are the biggest or most successful stars always seemed to be the most **likeable**. On several occasions, I found myself offering to help well-known stars as if these multi-millionaires, shouldered by a team of agents, managers, lawyers, publicists, business managers and partners, needed my assistance! But I couldn't help it. Their charm or likability was that hypnotic.

The lesson is clear: **Make them like you!** In order to do so, you must really dissect what it is likable and appealing about you. What behavior on your part would lead otherwise total strangers (who are no doubt hit on all the time for favors) to want to help you? You must continually analyze your behavior and modify it if it's not bringing you the desired results. Remember this, even in your schmoozing, you must be as distinctive and memorable as possible.

You Went There Too? Another effective schmoozing technique is to go **crazy with commonalities**. Bring upstate New York into a conversation with Michael Douglas and that may just be the "open sesame" to a conversation with someone who would otherwise prefer to walk away. What exactly do I have in common with the person I'm schmoozing?

At ICM, I found out that the red-hot Superman aka Christopher Reeve was a new client and tried to meet him. I was receiving many requests for him at the time. Chris didn't need to do this; he was making more than enough dough at the time from acting alone. And he told me so.

But I had done my research and happened to know that he was very passionate about the environment and the world. I told him he could speak on those topics if he wished. "I'll think about it. Thanks." Then I told him that we shared the same alma mater: Cornell University. We spoke about our related and respective experiences there. The beauty of its campus. The diversity of its student body. What it was like to act on stage in Ithaca, New York. Which of our classmates were also in the Biz. Within minutes, I was helping to represent Christopher Reeve.

Whether you are schmoozing in a social or business setting, you must do the math. What do you have in common with the person you're schmoozing? My late mother, Beverly, drilled this into my brother Stephen and my growing adolescent minds almost incessantly. In her pronounced and high-volume Bronx accent, she would bring up sketchy names, with whom we apparently shared something in common. When Stephen told her he was thinking about majoring in Chemical Engineering, he suddenly learned how many previously unknown offspring of our parents' friends were prospering in Chemical Engineering jobs. She dragged reluctant neighbors over to greet me when she discovered that they too were coin collectors! In later years, both of us would receive newspaper articles about those we happened to go to camp with or competed against in swimming meets.

Mom may have overdid it, but the point is you must immediately do your own brain scan and think of anything, however obscure, you may share with the person you're schmoozing. This is a brain search muscle you need to build. Do you share a similar hometown, high school, college, previous employer, hobby, ethnic background, travel destination, neighborhood?

If you discover you indeed have something in common, bring it up. It doesn't matter how insignificant the commonality, it is better than nothing. You can safely assume that a common conversational topic will be of greater interest to most than the weather or other generic topics. Most importantly, it may lead to a serious Eureka schmoozing moment.

Otherwise, you can always enhance your schmooze by contributing some fresh information or news: "There are now direct flights to Cape Town," or "The Wolverines definitely need a new football coach, don't you agree?" Or "They are casting for that film right now in New York." And you thought you had nothing to say.

Be overly familiar. This is not always so easy. For many of us, our natural inclination when meeting new and powerful people is to be stiff, formal, and distant. We tend to be nervous and unsure of ourselves. It is crucial to fight this tendency. Schmoozing is much more effective if you are **overly familiar**. To immediately proceed to the next step in getting to know the person and skip the initial formalities. Reminds me of that Barbara Streisand song, "Getting to Know You!"

Why? There is a simple reason: the more familiar you can be, the more likely your target person will want to engage in conversation, meet you again, or elevate your connection in some way (e.g. accept your script, allow you to pitch or audition, hire you, or introduce you to someone who is better suited to help you).

One can be overly familiar in a myriad of ways. If you have actually met this person before, trigger their memory or give them details before moving on to other conversational topics. Think of it as your conversational admission ticket. However memorable or unmemorable your prior meeting was, make sure to embellish it. By being on more familiar terms with the "schmoozee," you have a greater chance to benefit.

Mutual Somebody. Try to mention a mutual friend or acquaintance you may have in common. This is a superbly effective opening because it instantly qualifies you in their eyes. If this is not possible, it is not a capital crime to pretend that you have met them before. The more famous or successful the person, the more this technique will have traction because their schedule is insanely busy and they meet hordes of people.

There are other, perhaps more sincere ways of being overly familiar. If you have never met a person in common with them this in no way should hamper your ability to schmooze. You can always start the conversation with their latest art, film, or business accomplishment and mention how it had an impact on you and why. Again, try to be distinctive in expressing yourself.

For example, if you happen to meet Francis Ford Coppola, do you really have to praise "The Godfather?" Can you imagine how many times he has heard such comments? You will surely be much more memorable to him by praising his work in "Tucker." Try to make a personal connection if possible. Maybe your inventor uncle was inspired by the film to create his own vehicle. I don't know, but I can tell you this: successful people never tire of listening to such accolades.

I remember speaking with the late writer George Plimpton and mentioning his wonderful article on the first great travel writer, Richard Halliburton, one of my dad's favorite authors. This led to a lengthy conversation about the adventures of traveling. I had now snuck myself into a conversation and he was one hell of a conversationalist! **Don't be afraid to ask more and more familiar questions, which will erode the reality that this person was a complete stranger moments before.**

In your efforts to be an Olympian schmoozer, you are likeable, finding commonalities, overly familiar and are always **sincere, open, and vulnerable**. By being open and vulnerable you immediately intensify the schmooze. You also have a better chance of really connecting with the person in a meaningful way. This is because it allows you to step away from your role: asker, taker, aspiring or needy creative and leads you to becoming a real, red-blooded human being in the eyes of the "schmoozee." There can be no greater schmoozing goal.

But make sure you are authentic and genuine or this could backfire. Always, always, keep it real. Powerful people in the creative fields can read others quickly, an essential skill when meeting so many new people. As a result, they have incredible bullshit detectors. So please try to be your most sincere and memorable self.

While I was an entertainment agent at ICM, I was very eager to help represent the famous actress and author Shirley MacLaine. She was very busy but agreed to have lunch with me. I was not in my best form as I was going through a painful divorce at the time. My whole life perspective was distorted and I couldn't hide it, no matter how hard I tried.

As you can imagine, Shirley is extremely intelligent and intuitive. After a quick business chat, she asked what I was going through. I opened up to her and she clearly understood the misery of ending a relationship. She opened up to me in kind and discussed how and why relationships sometimes fail. How some of hers ended. Soon, we were on our way to an enjoyable agent-client relationship.

Being sincere, open and vulnerable is not only effective in schmoozing, but it is also a great avenue to improving your art and creativity. Are you opening up enough? Exposing your heart and soul? If not, what is stopping you? If you're a creative, you must know how important it is to avoid being inhibited or emotionally clogged. Let it out!

Make them laugh. Many of the best schmoozers happen to be damn funny. Really funny. But you don't have to be hysterical to be a great schmoozer. And even if being funny could be taught, which I don't believe possible, this book is simply not big enough. If you don't happen to be funny, please avoid forcing the issue with lame joke attempts. You know if you have this gift. If you do, USE IT!!

Seems obvious, right? But you can't believe how self-sabotaging funny people can be. They subvert their funny genes when they meet new people or those who may be useful to their careers. Their funny genes seem to hide or freeze. Don't let this happen to you. If you've got it, flaunt it. There is simply no better way to bond. Being funny could not be more distinctive and memorable. Not only will people remember you, but they'll probably want to be your friend as well. Or at least want to help you. And they'll rarely blow off your future calls.

All comedians aside, the funniest schmoozer I've ever talked to was Manny Azenberg, the legendary Broadway producer of dozens of Neil Simon shows, among others. At the time, Manny was representing Neil Simon's interests, and I desperately needed to speak to Mr. Simon. Not only did Manny allow this to happen, but, for fifteen minutes, he also made me laugh until I cried. I just wonder why this producer didn't write his own damn Broadway comedies— I'm sure they would've "killed."

The most effective schmoozers know when to charm and converse and when to **actively and attentively listen**. Unlike those funny genes that only some of us are blessed with, all of us have the potential to listen well. But many creatives live solitary lives during the day when we are creating. When we are out at night, we can't wait to talk our butts off. What is the next thing I'm going to say? Will it be a topic, story, or crack? Meanwhile the person you're schmoozing is speaking and you don't really hear him or her. You're too busy thinking of your next utterance.

I know an extremely talented artist in Boston, one who should have received far more recognition for his innovative photography, who simply can't shut up and let other people have the floor. It's like watching a Shakespearean soliloquy without the inner conflict. Monologue not dialogue. No pause whatsoever, just an endless gushing of words like a faucet that won't shut off. After a while, I become exhausted and happily leave his studio. Don't make this mistake! **Be in the moment and actively listen.** Not only is it the polite thing to do, but it also leads to a more engaging conversation--and a much more enjoyable exchange for the person you're trying to get to know. It opens the door to more mutual exciting conversational subjects, not just the ones you're fixated upon. This, of course, is schmoozing heaven.

Make yourself useful. Good schmoozing is a two-way street. Even though the person you are schmoozing may be famous or successful or they may have achieved the dreams to which you aspire, they don't owe you anything. Not one thing. Nada. If they're kind, maybe they help others once in a while, but there's no guarantee they'll help you. Please keep this in mind when you corner someone at a party or elsewhere. Try to avoid focusing solely on me, me, me. I want, I need, I take. What can you do for me? This behavior is clichéd, transparent and extremely annoying.

My brother Stephen and I once went to a party in Manhattan, where, I kid you not, the entire room of creatives was pitching their latest project. After some dude from Brooklyn went into a long diatribe about his brilliant screenplay, he then went on to give us the scene-by-scene rundown. Stephen and I just looked at each other and started laughing. We then went home and started writing a comedy sketch called, "The Pitch." Please, you need to be much more clever and considerate than this to be an Olympian schmoozer.

What Can I Do For You? One way that is incredibly effective is to simply ask "What can I do for you?" That's right. How can you help them? You would be surprised by the dozens of ways. If your conversation is proceeding well, figure out how you may be useful. What is your target presently working on? What is their next port of call? Do they need some scripts read or to find: a French-speaking actress, the best bookbinding place in New York, or a great restaurant in Houston. I don't know, but whatever their level of success, they're probably on the quest for something. What is their present Holy Grail? Or at minimum, their next errand to be done? It may not be possible, but be on the lookout if there is any way you can help.

Don't be afraid to be a connector. There may be someone exceptional in your social orbit you can introduce to this person, whether it's for professional or personal reasons. I still do this all the time for friends and family without any expectations. Sometimes even strangers. My brother's background as a travel writer is particularly useful in this regard. Especially with well-known actors who want to relax on a Caribbean or South Pacific island without the paparazzi snapping photos in their face. We give them a list of lesser known islands and resorts. **Call it good karma, but the more helpful you are, the more help comes your way. Try it and you'll see what I mean.**

Dating Etiquette. A delicate topic: Is it okay to actually date someone you're schmoozing? Someone who can help your career? The answer may surprise you. Absolutely, as long as your romantic interest is sincere and not used to advance your goals. It should not be conditional in any way. In fact, you shouldn't have any expectations about career enhancement, as they may not want to mix romance with business at all. Many of these people are extremely competitive—that's how they got to where they are. They may not want to "compete" with their significant other, comprende? Proceed cautiously but don't avoid such a romance unnecessarily—this could be the *one*. Numerous schmoozers have found their soul mate in the process of schmoozing.

All this romantic chatter is getting to my head. Whoa! Wooing and seduction are, indeed, closely related to schmoozing. True second cousins, if you ask me. Sincerity is effective in all of these pursuits.

So be yourself, open, vulnerable, and discuss topics of mutual interest. Listen actively and attentively. But, as they say in Turkey, Yavash, Yavash: slowly, slowly. Act in moderation. Those who are too obvious or who try too hard are destined to fail. Those who are in love with the sound of their own voice, those who put on airs or pretend be someone they are not, will not fare well. Those who are able to make a real, genuine connection; those who are likable and useful have an incredible advantage in schmoozing effectively.

Don't be overbearing. Let's say for argument's sake, your schmoozing did the trick and you are beginning an acquaintanceship or friendship with someone new who can actually help your career. Be cool, brother. You know what I'm saying? It's like high school, the more the person thinks you're chilled, the more of a future for the relationship.

Try to maintain a balanced approach to the person. A balanced give and take. Don't call or email too much. Don't be too needy or ask too much too often. Don't be in their face too much. Don't be a sycophant or a stalker in any way or you'll be discarded like yesterday's garbage.

All of us who have a modicum of success in this business have been approached by a plethora of eager and ambitious folks. Many of us try to help, sometimes even push them to the next plateau. But there is a sizable group who are clueless about how they come across. Their sense of entitlement may be oversized. Or they may feel their ambitions or goals must be fed at any cost. They are obnoxious and overbearing.

Such aspirants may lack social or emotional intelligence. They may not have an understanding or respect for maintaining reasonable personal boundaries. This is the quickest way for your fledgling relationship to be guillotined. Take a chill pill and read the hints the person is giving you. Accept his or her pace in the relationship, particularly if they are resisting yours. Let the relationship flow gently down the stream.

Practice, practice, practice. Now that you have a better idea of what good schmoozing is, this art still may be abhorrent to you. Please don't take this attitude as it is self-destructive--and maybe a potential career killer. Seriously. You must try to do it as much as you possibly can, and eventually, it will become easier. Maybe even enjoyable.

* * *

THE JOY OF INFORMATIONAL INTERVIEWS

Like many aspiring or working creative professionals, you may not have an agent or manager. If you are fortunate to have one or both, they may not be as effective as you would like. Indeed, most are only effective for a very small but profitable percentage of their clients. Perhaps, the top five percent of their income-producing clients.

The odds in this game can be frightening. Really frightening. Many aspiring and working creative professionals are in a rut. Their careers are simply frozen—and may have been for many years. Perhaps, they never really broke in. Or even more life-sapping, they had one major success and have not been able to parlay that into a consistent career or a steady income. They may admit it to themselves, rationalize like crazy or simply avoid this simple reality. Whatever tactic they use, it can become seriously frustrating. A strong dose of ambition and even entitlement can help propel you over the hump. And there are other tools to dig you out. One such tool that is often neglected: **Informational Interviews**.

Informational Interviews may require will, research and chutzpah on your part, but they can also yield absolutely amazing results. Basically, the world is your oyster. Anyone you want to meet is possible to meet. That's right—digest this please! Anyone you want to meet is possible. Of course, your chances are heightened if you happen to know someone who knows your target person. Indeed, in the age of Facebook and LinkedIn, you may be able to ascertain exactly whom you both know in common.

In addition, if you ever had any creative achievements or credits, your chances to meet whoever you want are greatly enhanced. Or if you ever held a position in the media or entertainment industries. If you lack both of these, don't despair--you can still succeed in meeting almost whoever you want in the business side of the arts, media and entertainment. **The only real failure is not to try. Yes, this is the biggest failure of them all.**

When I left ICM, I was a bit lost and confused. I really needed a break. Believe me, it is okay to feel lost and confused in your career journey or life. It happens now and then. Don't ever feel defeated by such feelings, particularly in such a difficult setting as the world of arts, entertainment or media.

I certainly knew I wanted to quit ICM. I had been doing it for way too long. Being an agent for me was intended as a brief stopover, a mere way station of my career, not a near decade-long tenure. After all, I had creative ambitions! I realized my tenure was almost over when I started to get jealous of my clients. Yes, I was doing well for them and my company, but I felt like I conquered this professional challenge. I wanted to go on—and take on an even greater challenge in the process.

What I didn't know at that time is whether I was going solely creative or continuing in a production executive/producer position--and letting my creative passions take a back seat again. I needed information and perspective. I needed to understand the lay of the land. I needed to figure out my career strategy and my future. I realize these are not the most optimal set of circumstances to arrange **Informational Interviews.** It would have been better to have already decided on my career goals.

Meeting Whomever You Want. If you are willing to be diligent and persistent, you have a chance of meeting almost whoever you want. The kings of industry, the titans of power, and the extremely successful. During a three week stretch in the mid-90's, I was able to meet the heads of four studios in addition to Norman Lear ("All in the Family" "Sanford and Son" "Who's the Boss"), Steven Bochco

("Hill Street Blues" "LA Law" NYPD Blue") and David E. Kelly ("Chicago Hope" "Ally McBeal" "Boston Legal"). These three furiously busy TV moguls were all exceptionally kind to me. Each spent over an hour with me sharing their experiences and giving their sage advice. For example, they all told me to write as much as possible, be disciplined and to be bold.

Remember, the competition is extreme. When I was growing up, my guidance counselor mother would often procure and place articles about creative career unemployment on the stairs leading to my bedroom. Often, these were bleak statistics from the Department of Labor or the unions themselves. I don't need to stick your face in the mud, but this calls for you to take occasionally courageous and original measures.

Informational Interviews: Operating Instructions: You first must find the phone numbers for those you want to speak to. With the web, particularly Google and IMDB Pro, you should be able to locate their office numbers. Whatever you do, never call your potential Informational Interviewees at home as it is an invasion of their privacy.

However, if their assistant is not putting you through, then I believe in the *open sesame* philosophy. That is, do whatever you have to do to reach your target without breaking the law. Tell their assistant that that they are expecting your call and if asked regarding what or which project, simply say "John or Mary knows." The reality is that most of these targets are so busy that they simply don't recall all the matters at hand, much less know all the people they have met. This reality may provide the open sesame you need!

The skill of cold calling or accessing someone successful without referencing a name can be extremely valuable to your career success. You can try my technique or develop your own. You may need to revise or modify your approach, but don't give up. Keep on trying different methods and you will eventually find your groove. Again, this may prove to be a useful and reliable skill for your entire career.

Before he was a giant name in show business, famed film producer and DreamWorks Animation CEO Jeffrey Katzenberg manned the phones for ICM Agent Sam Cohn, the legendary rep for Bob Fosse, Woody Allen, Mike Nichols, Meryl Streep, Robin Williams—to name a few. It was an almost impossible position as Cohn was particularly punishing if not sadistic to his assistants, especially his junior assistants. Ambitious even in this early stage of his career, Katzenberg eagerly accepted this challenge earning rare praise from his boss (which I also received as Cohn chewed paper) who was impressed at his long hours, enthusiasm, and his early ability to get anyone on the line. Indeed this was how Katzenberg got the job in the first place. He got Cohn on the line—a nearly impossible feat—and asked for a job.

My Technique. So give it a shot. Create whatever pretense or excuse you want, but get your target on the line. You may have to call four or five times. Accept this at the start. As mentioned elsewhere in this treatise, 95% of those in show business are insecure however lofty their position. Therefore, when speaking to your target, you need to simply appeal to their ego. Be authentic and sincere if possible! Praise one or two of their achievements or credits. Tell them how much they or their work has inspired you. Just don't go over the top as these people can smell bullshit a mile away. Charm and praise will go a long way in your life and career. Seems overly simple but, if delivered in a genuine way, it works!

Then immediately tell the person that you would really love to meet them for advice "anytime and any place." That it will be brief- -just ten or fifteen minutes. "I would really appreciate 'getting your career advice' or 'picking your brain.' If you want to lay it on strong, you could resort to "surely you received advice on your way up" or something like that, but you probably won't need to. Typically, if you appeal to their ego (but avoid overdoing it), they will give you some time. And meet with you. There are numerous reasons for this, but usually, it is because they have received random advice, kindness and even mentoring early in their careers and feel an obligation to do the same for others. Or they thoroughly understand karma. Or both. Some may have a particular soft spot for young or aspiring creative professionals but **Informational Interviews also work for those working creative professionals of any age aspiring to the next plateau**.

Meet in Person! However busy your target is, never consent to just an email exchange or solely a phone conversation if you can help it. Your intention is get your Informational Interviewee to help you directly or indirectly. Now is the time you need them! **Learn how to ask for help!** This is much, much easier in person. Strive to meet your target in person.

Face-to-face meetings are exponentially more effective. It's basic common sense—if your meeting target happens to like you, they'll do that much more for you. If you impress them and passionately ask for help, they may even hire or represent you or refer you to someone who will.

Primary and Secondary Contacts. Back to **Primary Contacts** or those successful contacts that can help you the most. These are the creative big shots who could hire you or buy your creative labor right now! Or could represent you in such pursuits. For an actor, this would be an agent, manager, casting director, producer, and last but certainly not least, director. For a thorough list of **Primary Contacts**, peruse the **Networking System Chapter**.

As you know, **Secondary Contacts** are those powerful or connected souls who are one iPhone or Blackberry text or phone call away from the **Primary Contacts**. In other words, they know them! Or have some connection with them. **Secondary Contacts** are in a tangential field that interacts or overlaps with those **Primary Contacts.** In an actor's context, this could include: advertising and public relations executives, theater artistic directors, recording or publishing executives, journalists, college professors, acting teachers, cinematographers, or many other positions. They may not be able to hire or represent you directly, but they know the ones who can.

The main challenge with **Secondary Contacts** is to get them to cough up some **Primary Contacts** that can help you now. Once they've given you some names, you need to be aware of the best case scenario for them to help you in this regard. In other words, what are the best results you can hope to achieve?

Be Specific! Whether an Informational Interview or any other type of meeting, when meeting someone who is better known or more experienced than you, perhaps, an amazing connection or someone who can help you, it is always better to be as specific as possible. Then their advice is much more targeted and catered to you and your specific situation. Their advice is much more usable.

When meeting a contact, again **be as specific in your requests as possible.** "Can you get me in front of Ms. Stern, your casting director?" or "I'd love to get a writing assignment with Vanity Fair," or "Can you connect me to the literary agent of your last book?" This is not the time to act too cool, aloof, or intentionally vague. Celebrities can act like this on television talk shows after they've made it. But believe you me, they didn't act this way when they were struggling to make it. They learned how to ask for help! So can you. Show your passion and learn how to state your specific need.

* * *

NETWORKING HIERARCHY

Let's say you have succeeded in meeting with a **Primary** or **Secondary Contact**. You may actually know them. Or you may have something in common with them or not. What is the next step? **If you're with a Primary Contact, you try to get them to hire, represent or invest in you. In the office—before you leave!** You generally do this by getting them to see, read or otherwise evaluate your talents.

Unfortunately, many Primary Contacts may be way out of your league or strata. They're simply too big for you. That is, they have spent a lifetime meeting those in your creative profession and you would be in the caboose of a very long line. If this is the case, what to do? Get them to spill out some names! Particularly those who are closer to your strata or even those who know people who are more likely to be interested Primary Contacts or Secondary Contacts.

As I mentioned before, if you are meeting Secondary Contacts, try to convince them to connect you with Primary Contacts. Boldly ask which Primary Contacts your Secondary Contact knows. Literally get him or her to cough up names if you can. They'll usually spit out a few. If they are secretive or guarded, you may want to simply ask if they know any agents or managers or other Primary Contacts based on your creative goals.

Once your Secondary Contact mentions Primary Contacts, you are ready to put into action my **Networking Hierarchy**.

The best, absolute best result you can achieve is for the Secondary Contact to arrange for you (and them) to meet and socialize with one or more Primary Contacts directly. Let's say Secondary Contact Sam calls Primary Contact Peter. "Hi Peter, Sam here. Are you free to meet to have drinks with my new friend Jim here and me next Tuesday?" Nothing beats this option, but you usually have to know the Secondary Contact well for this to happen.

The next best option is to have them make a call on your behalf to meet the Primary Contact they know. "Hey Peter, would you mind meeting my new friend Jim here?"

The third best option is for the Secondary Contact to allow you to use their name in calling a Primary Contact they know. "Hi Peter, I'm Jim Jermanok calling at the suggestion of your friend Sam. I would love to meet you…"

The fourth best option is to use their name anyway without their permission. Yes, you read this correctly. Who exactly are you hurting? And you can always phrase it in a way to avoid lying. For example, "I was speaking to Sam and he spoke so highly about you." Get it? I'm not crazy about this last option, but I'd rather you make progress than be stopped dead in your tracks. Let's not allow stingy, unhelpful people to get the upper hand!

Chain of Contacts. It is crucial for you to understand that sometimes there is a long chain of contacts you will have to meet before you meet someone who will really make a difference. Someone who will actually do something for you.

For example, let's say you meet Sam or A, who will suggest that you meet Peter or contact B, as well as contacts C and D. Peter or Contact B and Contact C don't do a thing besides wish you good luck. However, Contact D likes you and introduces you to E, F, and G. E won't meet you no matter what. F tells you stories of his or his ascent but is stingy with introducing you to a primary contact. Contact G, however, is willing to represent or hire you. So it took from contact A to G for something good to happen.

These contact chains are standard in creative careers. Please play them out and be patient. There is often a long line of talented creatives who are in front of you. Patience really is a virtue in making a living creatively. So you might have to work the chain to contact X to make something happen, but man will you be psyched when it does.

In meeting chains of contacts, once again, there are contacts who may simply not be ready for you. You have not professionally ripened enough for their liking. They will tell you to call when you reached a milestone, say acted in a Broadway show, when your script is being produced into a film, or when you're having a big art gallery show. You may ask yourself why you'll ever need such a contact at that point, but it's foolish to insult or discard them.

The Boundary of Obnoxiousness Is Much Farther Than You Think. Many of us creatives defeat or sabotage ourselves right out of the gates. Don't ever avoid meeting people who you need to meet to obtain creative success because of fear. Don't ever shy away from trying to make your creative career happen or gain traction because of cowardice. Or the mistaken belief that trying to network or ask for help is obnoxious or... here's another defeatist word, improper. The hell with impropriety! What exactly is proper? Again, the competition is insane and hard to fathom.

The fence, border or boundary of obnoxiousness is so much farther in this business than you think. Be bold and aggressive in asking people to help you. Remember this: If you are talented, then you're doing them (and the world) a favor by aggressively serving your talents.

* * *

WHO ARE YOUR MENTORS?

Whether you're pursuing a creative living on your own or within a organizational structure, having your very own **mentor** is an amazing catalyst to making a creative living. Merriam-Webster defines mentor as "someone who teaches or gives help and advice to a less experienced and often younger person." It is generally someone several notches above you in terms of experience or accomplishment. It could be someone who is several levels above you in a company or one who has simply achieved what you are trying to achieve. In short, they have done it.

Mentors are nothing short of essential for creative career success. They can push you through that seeming force field to the next plateau. They can analyze what you're doing right and what you're doing wrong. They can guide you if you've lost your way or have slowed down for any reason—and there are many of them. Their achievements can inspire you to do what they did, particularly if you've lost your faith in actualizing your goals.

Mentors can also introduce you to Primary Contacts—those that can hire, represent or invest in you! They can lend their superb reputation to enhance yours. Indeed, they can also tutor you about how to act with these contacts to your best advantage. They can also advise you on so many matters: which projects or paths to pursue, which people to avoid, and how to resolve problems that inevitably arise in a creative career.

Some creative professionals are very fortunate to already have mentors in their life. That's right, someone who is already making a very successful creative living—who happens to like and respect you. They are established, generous and wise with their suggestions.

They sincerely want you to succeed. For these lucky few, it may be a family member like an uncle or older brother. Or it could also be a friend or family friend. This is a Godsend, of course, but is rarely the case unless you happen to grow up in LA, NY or London.

For the rest of us, we are tasked with **finding and keeping our own mentors**. The first thing you should know is that this is absolutely possible, but may require some serious effort on your part. Is there anyone in your company, anyone you may have worked with, anyone with whom you may have had an informational interview-- who you feel a kinship with? Whatever the difference in your levels of attainment, maybe there is a serious connection or bond between you and your potential mentor. You may both be from the same university, acting or art school; same hometown, state or country. **Or you may have similar world views, personalities, or senses of humor—it doesn't matter, but those with whom you have some personal or demographic bond are your most likely prospects.**

When you have figured out who may be your potential mentors, the next step is to try to be their friend or fond acquaintance. Is there something, perhaps a project of your own design, you can help them with? Can you assist them to achieve their latest goals somehow? Is there anyone or any group you can bring to their attention? Any new source of income or financing or promotion/success you can introduce them to? Is there something you can personally do to make their life easier or more successful? Any new website or social media platform you can offer to promote their latest book, film, or play? Is there a film or theater premiere, book or art opening you can invite them to? Is there a new opportunity or a new someone you can introduce to them? There must be something you can do for them!

These same skills and benefits will also help you maintain or keep a mentor once they've agreed, however openly or unofficially, to be your mentor. **Don't stop being a benefit or, better yet, a friend to your mentor**. If you ask too much or do not reciprocate to the best of your ability and contacts, you may push them away. Having a mentor is ideally a two-way street. **Be as useful to them as they are to you**.

A caveat: Try to avoid starting the initial mentor sourcing too quickly. The more successful or prominent your potential mentor is, the stronger their antennae for being used, the more they are aware of ambitious people trying to take advantage of them. Instead, get to know them gradually, try to help them gently—as if it were the mentor's idea. Don't get me wrong, you need to be ambitious and somewhat calculated to succeed--but clever in how you conceal these qualities. For example, you don't have to unload all of your exact career goals in your first sitting. As you get to know each other, you can layer on information (like in a good script) that clarifies your talent and goals.

Praising your mentor is also an excellent tactic, but it should be sincere because, once again, their higher level of achievement required excellent bullshit detecting and people reading abilities. All of us creatives love praise and compliments for a variety of reasons, just make sure you know what you're talking about. Do the necessary research! If your potential mentor believes you, he or she will like you more—and hopefully develop an interest in both you and your work.

Asking for advice. When you think you are ready; when you've known your potential mentor for a while, **another effective way to mold them into your mentor is to simply ask them for advice**. It may be about making a choice between two possibilities, dealing with a nasty executive at the company or answering a entertainment question like how to get distribution for your film or how to write a great book proposal. Better yet, ask for personal advice if you think it is not too intrusive. The act of giving or receiving advice is, in itself, a form of bonding. It is a form of feeding and fulfilling each other's best human qualities and should result in an enhanced relationship.

Eventually, it will be time for you to show your mentor your talent, whatever form it takes. Of course, if you are both working on a project together, this is not necessary because they already have a front row seat to observe your abilities. Otherwise, you need them to take the time to evaluate your talents. If you are an artist or musician, it is much easier for your mentor to digest than if you happen to be a novelist or screenwriter, for example. Really make sure your mentor is ready or adequately invested to read your script or manuscript--as it requires many hours away from their busy schedules.

Rejection. You may be rejected by your mentor at any time. Try not to take it personally. Your potential mentor may not have the time or maybe they don't want to help anyone but themselves— yes, some successful creatives are just too self-involved to really care about the careers of others, but thank God, this is rare. The solution: Don't be discouraged—try again with them within a month.

There is also the possibility that your potential mentor may appreciate your talents but will not take any steps to helping you improve or succeed. Thus, there is a disconnect between their appreciation of your talents and their actions to help further your career. Unfortunately, this is way too common. If this happens to you, simply try to ask for specific help later on. For example, "Can you please get this to the attention of your friend, the literary agent?"

If you try these tactics and are still are rejected, don't despair as this mentor may come around in time. Again, don't be discouraged. Your mentor may have their fill of "mentees" or not have the time for another connection of any type. It probably has nothing to do with you or your talents! Stop attempting to analyze the reason(s) behind the rejection—and pursue other potential mentors at once!

Is there a mentor you can convert from your newest creative group? From your latest meeting or project? Someone close to a family member or good friend? A mentor who belongs to your alumni or professional association? Perhaps, someone in your social or social media sphere that you can get to know better? The point is to not give up in your pursuit of a mentor or two—they can definitely accelerate your making a living creatively, if not change your life.

* * *

ESSENTIAL HEAD STARTS TO GALVANIZING YOUR CREATIVE CAREER

As many of you are well aware, getting your film, play, TV or web series made is often as easy as playing hopscotch in a minefield. Yet, sometimes we're too close to the forest to see the trees. Or is it too close to the trees to see the forest? Whatever the idiom, you and your creative or production team might have overlooked an amazing advantage. A head start that may save you numerous years in getting your project made! Someone in your life or social orbit who can make the difference. Or it could be your birthplace, birth country, background or project that could alone be the tipping point.

Although this chapter is geared toward those of you who have wares, meaning something to make, film or sell, all of you can benefit from the following head starts.

Head Starts

Knowing a Star. Seems so simple and obvious, right? But I'm often surprised at how many actors, filmmakers, writers and producers are afraid to ask for help from celebrities. Maybe you don't want to bother your star buddy, but I assure you that they asked a whole bunch of people for help before they succeeded. They may seem smooth and relaxed now in talk shows and magazine interviews, but most pushed, prodded, coaxed and utilized every contact they had on their way to riches. An unfortunate caveat here: there may only be a brief window or tenure for their stardom and corresponding clout. After that fades, they may well be asking for your help.

A star (and it doesn't need to be a movie star; a TV star, recording star or sports star will do) can, of course, be the lead in your film or play. That probably won't happen unless you're best friends or well known yourself, but what if he or she appears in a supporting or cameo (brief) role? Or better yet, they could direct your film or play. Guess what? **Suddenly all of their network is now your network for all intents and purposes.** You'll meet almost all of their important entertainment friends and contacts. How's that for serious contact accumulation?

Not going to happen? Don't despair. If they really like your script or play, there is one more option—get them onboard to produce or executive produce your project. Even if they simply present or lend their name (in film it is a coveted cottage industry that has benefited such directors as Francis Ford Coppola, Martin Scorsese and Spike Lee--to name a few) to it, that's a huge boost in separating your film or play from the rest of the ever increasing pack.

Knowing a Prominent or Name Director. In the world of film, having the right director can bring rapid or certainly easier financing. As you may have figured out, these very busy humans are in great demand. If the director you know has "meaning" (funding potential) to film distributors or sales agents and, if the film can attract presales (pre-financing in exchange for a territorial rights) or other forms of investment--by all means, send them the script at once. Ask him or her to direct! It is a head start that could transform your career, get you an elusive feature film credit and save you many years of financing hell.

Unfortunately, many of the name or A-list directors are booked years in advance, but there is still a chance as films collapse often even for directors of this caliber. There is also another category of financeable directors—those who don't like to commit too far in the future. Get your director chum to read your script. Once again, if they like your project, they can also produce with you. Simply attaching their name (not to mention accompanying personal endorsement) to your project will draw a lot more interest.

Knowing a TV Showrunner/Executive Producer. The same enhancement goes for reality or fictional television, but in this field, the showrunner or executive producer is king. Usually these folks are former line producers in reality television and writer-producers in fictional television. They are the chosen people for network or cable television. Those capable figures that the network and cable television executives trust to produce shows on time and under budget.

Having a Showrunner attached to a TV project is a huge head start to getting it greenlit or financed. For reality or unscripted shows, better make sure that the brief sizzle reel (2-5 minute trailer of what your program will look like) is distinctive and compelling along with a concise proposal. In fiction, that pilot script better rock. For both, having a name actor or host can push it over the edge to success.

Knowing a Producer—Which brings us to another film and theater king: Producers. As discussed before, it is important to stratify yourself and your project with producers. Know their genre and budget preferences—that is, their specific producing sweet spots. My usual advice is to only approach those producers whose preferred genres, mediums and budgets are damn close to what you're going for.

However, if you happen to be friends with a certain producer, by all means, present your project to them. They may really like the script. Even if they are commonly pigeonholed (essentially forced to work in the medium or genre that they first succeeded) in the market, producers are generally much more versatile and diverse than commonly believed. You never know if he or she will help you out. God knows, it could open up doors for them. They may enjoy the break from their usual fare.

There is also the possibility of them simply supporting your project as an advisor, mentor or executive producer. In other words, they can play a less demanding or secondary role than being lead producer. This may provide a restful interlude for them. It also allows them to aid a deserving talent, friend or family member. It doesn't get better than that, does it?

Knowing a Financier—Do you know a Venture Capitalist, Hedge Fund Executive, or Private Equity Executive? Hel-lo! Knock Knock!! I don't care if they are not in the business. I don't care if they detest theater or the arts. It doesn't matter if they don't know Quentin or Oliver from a hole in the head. They can really help you!

Reluctance often precedes assistance. These people are hit on all the time for investment in non-creative or less risky businesses and start-ups. They may state that they're "in a completely different industry" or "lack expertise in film or theater investment altogether" but don't let this detract you. Or let them off the hook.

These whizzes are experts at financing, which is precisely what you need to get your film or theater project off the ground. Although they may not have specific, hands-on experience investing in entertainment, media, or the arts, they most certainly know a wide range of investors who have--and may be game to do so again. They also know a number of new or better yet, nouveau riche investors who may be willing to give it a shot for the first time. On top of that, a number of hedge and private equity funds maintain "alternative investments" sections, which can be appealing, particularly in a flat or bear market.

Being Rich. Congratulations. You know who you are. You're one of the lucky ones who have wealthy parents or family, a trust fund or even a self-made successful business. Don't despair, you don't have to fully finance your film or entertainment project, but it certainly would help if you put some money in it. Most film or theater equity investors do not want to be the first to invest in a project for a variety of reasons, primarily perceived risk. So your contribution would definitely solve that problem. Plus, all the equity investors I've ever met simply love it when the lead producer, director or filmmaker has skin in the game.

Still not parting with your wallet? One more caveat: If any of your potential investors discover that you are a person of "means" and have not put money into your own darn artistic project, they will be (pick one) furious, suspicious and/or awfully reluctant to invest.

Knowing Someone Rich. Whether they are family or a friend to you, it is certainly worth a shot. You'd surprised on how hesitant or shy creatives can be in this area. "I'll ask them on my second film." Or "I just don't want to bother them." I hear you but I just want you to understand how difficult financing any project can be. To avoid anyone you're close to who has money simply does not make sense. Why load yourself with needless additional (or countless) years of pursuing money if you know a rich someone who can give you an early boost?

Here are a few other factors to ponder. Depending on their wealth, you won't be the first (or the last) artist to ask them for money. They are used to it. Maybe you'll be the one to convince them to say yes. Still not swayed? How would you feel if you don't ask and they end up investing with a complete stranger, mere acquaintance, or, God forbid, a mutual friend? Go for it!

They don't have to pay for the entire film or play. Once again, it is terribly difficult to *break the ice*—to get that first investor to invest. Perhaps, your rich family member or friend can make that first investment and start the momentum. Or you can attract an initial investment and then ask them to match it. You can also ask them for the all too precious finishing funds that have defeated far too many films, docs, and shorts.

Like any other potential investor, never ever deceive them about the riskiness of such an investment. Make no mistake, these are risky investments, but they are giving you an enormous career boost, contributing to art and culture, and, I promise, making one of the most enjoyable investments they ever made. Give it a shot!

Be Specific. As with **Primary** or **Secondary Contacts**, once again **Be Specific**! This is a particularly important piece of advice when asking favors from well-known, successful or wealthy contacts. Most of these people tend to be insanely busy so you need to be as specific and prepared as possible. Unless you're extremely close, try to avoid asking for general help. They don't have the time (or often, willingness) to figure out how to help you. Also, many of these contacts don't fully understand how they themselves succeeded. They may not have a clue about how they can help you. So make it easy for them! **Be specific!** You must make the task of helping you as easy and user-friendly as possible!

If you have specific name(s) of exactly whom you'd like to meet, it is always easier for your head start contact to comply!

Do the research! For example, if you are an actor and your actor or director friend is on a television series, **do the research!** Find out who is the casting director and ask your friend if they can arrange a meeting. Or if you or your agent can call the casting director directly.

If you are a director and trying to fund a film, find out if your financial friend can arrange a meeting between you and any investor friends who may be inclined to invest in the arts. Once again, it is incumbent on you to do the research (e.g. on their social media platforms) and figure out which of their friends/contacts would be most likely to have strong interest.

In the workshops I do worldwide, I often ask my happy participants to yell out their successful or famous contacts by occupation. I don't need to know their names. Then I ask what creative career my audience members are pursuing--and quickly connect the dots. Are they describing primary or secondary contacts? Can they invest, represent or hire you immediately or they simply know those who do? If they can't directly hire you, then who in their company, crew, team, or social orbit can? Do the research and make your contact's assistance less of an effort. The easier it is for them, the more of a chance such a connection will happen, understand?

Research is an extremely important component of creative career success.

If you are not that experienced as a researcher, now is the time to get your hands dirty. It is not advanced astrophysics, I can assure you. Just go to Google or Bing and read many, if not all, of the relevant article links that appear. Are there any articles about them in the popular press, industry publications or blogs? If your friend/contact is in film, go to imdb.com. If they're in Hollywood, try searching on deadline.com or the trades: online *Hollywood Reporter* or *Variety*. If your contact is British or European, try ScreenDaily.com.

Once again, you can do a serious social media analysis, particularly, if you are connected on LinkedIn, Facebook, Twitter, and Google+.

Are there any mutual friends/contacts you can call to ask about the subject of your inquiry? You know, engage in basic interviews like a journalist or non-fiction author would—except sometimes, you may have to hide the reality that you are "interviewing." Another benefit, all these forms of research usually lead to other potential connections.

More Head Starts

Having business or legal experience. It is amazing how many creative professionals have extensive business or legal backgrounds that they don't draw upon. Maybe they want to shed that part of their life as a new creative professional. Or, for some reason, they feel inferior in applying such skills to the entertainment business.

I get that the entertainment, media and art businesses may seem intimidating, particularly to newcomers. But having these skills is an enormous head start compared to your creative competitors who lack them altogether, those who may be vying for the same job or career. Although it is crucial to have a specialized entertainment attorney and preferably experienced producers on your team, your business or legal chops can also make the difference in making a living creatively.

Those who are blessed with such experience also understand that that show business is, in many ways, like any other business. Sales, marketing, publicity, negotiation and executing contracts is of utmost importance. If you possess these skills, use them to your advantage! Complement and contribute to your business team. Use these skills to get to the finish line faster. It may not happen without you.

Having a foreign passport. Don't get me wrong. It is not easy to make a creative living anywhere. Wherever you're pursuing your creative career, it will require all of the skills and practices described in this primer. However, in many countries, there is a lot more government support than in America. Yes, we have the paltry budget of the Endowment of the Arts (whose funds may be harder to access than the lottery), and there are a few foundations and grants around, but nothing like Canada and many of the European and Asian countries. Thus, almost every American creative is trying to be hired or financed by the same small group of media corporations and the ever decreasing number of private equity investors or collectors. **Welcome to American Financial Darwinism.**

Our great neighbor to the north has a government that is much more supportive of the arts. For example, if you're Canadian and trying to finance a film, play or art project, you can apply for funding from the federal, provincial and even municipal governments! Sometimes, more than one province will subsidize.

When it comes to film, you can receive the above funding as well as monies from the government of one of the over 100 countries worldwide with which Canada has film co-production treaties. That's right, you can obtain funding from Canada and let's say the UK or Australia. Sometimes, you can receive tri-lateral funding from the governments of three or more countries. The US is one of the few countries in the world that doesn't have these film or artistic co-production treaties. Let's hope this changes.

In Europe or Asia, a native filmmaker can also receive funding from similar sources available to a Canadian in addition to continental funding from an organization like the MEDIA Program, part of the European Union, or the Asian Cinema Fund.

To recap, if you have a foreign passport or if you are eligible for a foreign passport (what's stopping you?), investigate which subsidies and funding programs you may benefit from. Even if you weren't planning on returning home so soon, it may be much easier to obtain support in your home country than to thrust yourself in competition for the dwindling sources of private financing in America at present.

Your Work Is Branded. Forgive me for adding to the litany of literature around the white-hot word, *branding*. But make no mistake; having a film, TV series or play that is branded is an extraordinary head start. By brand, I don't mean my dad's company for 40 years, *GE*, although it is conceivable. No, I mean any link to your play or script—well-known author, personality, concert, holiday, website, magazine, well-known TV show, foreign country, historical incident, war, sport, activity or hobby—that will attract a pre-existing and hopefully, substantial audience. Got it?

This is why Hollywood is currently in love with comic book

heroes, bestselling young adult books, video games, famous novels and sequels, sequels, sequels. This is why Broadway loves revivals. This is why television loves copying or modifying other television hits (e.g. *American Idol* turns into *The X Factor* and *The Voice*). **There is a pre-existing (and excited) audience that the studio, network, distributor or theater company doesn't have to create from scratch. Much of their marketing has already been done for them. So if there is an inherent branding potential in your project, this is an extreme head start. Run with it.**

It is imperative to be aware of all the assets and strengths your film, TV show or play has going for it. **Equally important is a list of your powerful friends and colleagues whose impact may prove to be the head start you need to make your production happen!**

* * *

SURVIVAL JOBS

Until you are able to support yourself make a living creatively, guess what? You need to survive or pay your monthly bills, commonly known as your "nut." Do you know the amount of your monthly nut? Take three months of bills and come up with an average. That's right—add them up and divide by three! This nut cannot be paid on hope or wishful thinking alone. Thus, you need to make a decision: Will you try to get a job in the creative business or one of a variety of **Survival Jobs**?

The advantage of **Survival Jobs** is that, ideally, you are free to focus on your craft exactly when you want to. Generally, these positions (with some notable exceptions like Administrative Assistant and Entrepreneur below) are less draining, intellectually and otherwise. They leave your artistic mind clear and more creatively fertile. Hopefully, less headaches, worries or clutter in your head. Less stress or there should be.

You don't want to be consistently reminded about how you are doing compared to those incredibly successful creative professionals or icons whom you are selling, promoting or working with. This can be a gnawing problem for many. Why? Because how well these creative successes are doing illuminate what many fragile souls see as their own lack of creative career progress.

For peace of mind and happiness, never ever compare yourselves to others you perceive as more successful.

Survival Jobs also allow more flexibility in your schedule so you can go to meetings, auditions, and other important events without too much of a hassle. Many of your bosses/owners are used to employing creatives and will permit you to modify your schedule within reason. They also understand when you get a creative job and will adjust your schedule to accommodate you. If they refuse and you lose your job, it is easier to deal with because it is less of a hassle to obtain a similar Survival Job again—relative to those precious jobs on the business side of your craft. Since Survival Jobs are more plentiful, the notion of job security is not as important as with jobs on the business side of the craft.

Once again, the goal of Survival Jobs is to pay your nut, change your schedule with ease, endure less stress and intellectual drain. If this is not possible, then leave your Survival Job immediately and find another one!

Here is my take on a number of Survival Jobs in no particular order:

1. Administrative Assistant to Lawyers or Bankers. Great pay—can be 80-200G. Very long hours and limited flexibility to modify your schedule. Can be very stressful and entail numerous responsibilities.   Bosses can be overly demanding and inconsiderate. Great job to park yourself for a few years and save like crazy. Good for writers and authors if you can motivate yourself to work during your limited leisure—weeknights and weekends. Will learn about contracts and meet a host of potential investors—you never know.

2. Barista. Very relaxed environment unless there's a stampede of customers. Flexible hours unless you own the place, which may be preferable. Will interact with useful connections if you happen to bond with them. Nights are generally free but hours usually begin very early. Unless you're totally into coffee, you may become resentful of overly demanding coffee addicts.

3. Blogger/Journalist/Web Content Provider. If this is your end goal, please forgive me as these can be amazing lifelong jobs. However, these positions are also great ways to support yourself for other creative pursuits if you happen to write well. Not to mention a great stepping stone—e.g. there are numerous Variety and Hollywood Reporter journalists who reinvented themselves are screenwriters, directors and producers. Complete control over your schedule. Great business experience if you're involved in promotion and pricing. Being an expert on a specific field will always attract a following. Added bonus of meeting potential primary contacts and investors.

4. Entrepreneur. To own your own business is an amazing choice that can be income-producing for your entire life. You will have total control over your schedule and personnel. To be successful usually requires three to five years of long and all-consuming hours to get it off the ground. It always takes much, much longer than you think. Try to hire a manager or right-hand person to delegate when you need the time to work on and promote your creative craft. Your business expertise and skills will, of course, transfer to your creative pursuits—if you let them.

5. Family Business. Good money but you may have to work with family or relatives you don't want to see on a daily basis—or you can only bear in short doses. They should be understanding about your schedule but you never know. Increasing pay and family pressure may force you to stay much longer than anticipated. But what's more important than familia, right? Let's take that blood oath right now!

6. Import/Export. Not an easy job to obtain, but can develop amazing wheeling-dealing skills—very useful in making future creative projects happen. If you can figure out who is looking for that surplus of Chinese cement, close the deal, do the shipping and insurance details, you're off to the races. Could be a financial pool you can dip your toe in throughout your career. Excellent training for producers—you will be operating under pressure and putting out your share of fires. Great international business experience.

7. Paralegal/Proofreader. Steady and salaried income usually in a chilled, classy environment. Depending on your boss, may be able to modify your schedule now and then. Some bosses are known to be tyrants or assholes—or, if you like, tyrannical assholes. Surprise, surprise, some lawyers can be insanely condescending—don't let it get to you. Others are surprisingly supportive. Many of my close friends are esquires. Not enormous stress unless there is a huge case happening.

8. Receptionist/Security Guard/Parking Attendant. Good steady employment, but must be able to deal with random, bothersome members of the public. Interest in reading or thinking for hours on end is a plus. Countless hours of idleness must not be alienating. Must be nice to bosses although they might not be nice to you. Advancement is rare but do you really care?

9. Real Estate Broker. Another job where you have to deal with an often demanding and annoying public. A very competitive if not cutthroat situation, especially when you begin. Must be a real independent go-getter. Excellent to hone your sales and negotiating skills. You will gradually resent how much more the boss/company is making. Control over your schedule and big earnings potential.

10. Salesperson. Great training for the future when you will be continually selling yourself and your creative projects. Generally, control over your schedule. Must be comfortable being alone. Although it is great preparation for your creative future, you must learn how to cope with repeated rejections. Pay can be risky and there is a trend of forcing salespeople to be 1099's or independent contractors (and pay for their own benefits while being denied future unemployment benefits if needed). Incredible boredom if you lack interest in the product—or, sometimes, even if you have interest.

11. Taxi/Limo Driver. Only if you are truly at ease with driving 8-12 hours per day. Patience is a virtue during traffic jams and idleness. Decent money and the opportunity to meet a diverse cross-section of the public. Can be dangerous (criminal passengers, cops, and traffic accidents, etc.) on many levels. Some fellow drivers can be catty and competitive.

12. Temp. Harder to obtain in a contracting economy. Usually a rather chilled experience but they don't tolerate many schedule changes. May have to hide your creative dreams. Occasionally can lead to a full-time job. Several agencies specialize in the arts and media, but this may not be what you want. Bosses can be very condescending and some tasks are mind-numbingly monotonous.

13. Teacher/Professor. Generally a very soulful and satisfying activity to educate others. Great to make a difference in the world and to help others on their way. You will always hone and expand your area of expertise. Depending on supervisory personnel, there can be nasty politics now and then. Some departments are receptive to improving curricula, others are overprotective and defensive. Intensive teaching or lecturing is surprisingly draining. Can modify your schedule if submitted far enough in advance. Added bonus: If you keep your ears open, you will always learn from your students. Always.

14. Tutor. Numerous job opportunities, particularly to tutor middle school and high school students. SAT/ACT tutoring is an industry in itself. Some opportunities to actually tutor your craft, whether it be: art, music, acting, writing or singing. Total control over your hours, good pay and a relaxed environment. Must be very patient, tolerant (e.g. spoiled teenagers) and understanding or you may lose it.

15. Waiter/Bartender. Ok, I'm not the foremost expert as I was fired from a number (actually a dozen) of waiting/bartending jobs before I kept one for a while. If you pick the right place, you can make serious money and even meet useful contacts in your field. Bosses can be sadistic. High turnover so you can find one of these positions with relative ease. Be prepared to embellish your resume if you've had limited experience--what's the worse that could happen?

16. Webmaster/IT Expert. Requires serious education and experience. Great way to control your hours and gain experience in sales, promotion and negotiation. Very valuable to become a maven and expert. Can focus on those already prominent in your industry, which could be very helpful. If you are proficient and popular, can almost name your fee. May be able to obtain consulting work for Primary Contacts and their companies. Can also barter for favors from those in your chosen creative field.

Staying the course. It is up to you to stay your creative course and keep your dreams alive! Whether you obtain a job on the business side of your craft or choose a Survival Job, you must always keep aware of what you need to do to succeed creatively. This will require organization, time management, intense efforts, drive and extraordinary discipline. Don't get down on yourself if you don't always accomplish your scheduled tasks as planned. You may not always have the time each week to do everything you want. Make sure to make time to think and prioritize. Try to do what you can to hone your craft and network with those Primary Contacts, the important people who can help accomplish your creative goals and reach the next level.

* * *

JOBS TO JUMPSTART YOUR CAREER

You read it about it all the time in Variety and Hollywood Reporter. Frank, the low man on the totem pole at a production company, who works as a humble script reader, suddenly writes his own script and sells it for hundreds of thousands of dollars. Or the production assistant at the music video production company who befriends the lead singer of a hot band and is chosen to direct their next video. Or the art gallery assistant who sells her own work to the visiting mega-collector.

Work for an independent film or production company, film studio, television network, entertainment agency, film festival, public relations company, art gallery; or as an assistant to a well-known star, director or producer and you just may have the inside track to achieving your dream. Or will you be turned off to a creative career path forever?

As discussed in the **Later Lessons Chapter**, I think it is a tremendous advantage if you can stomach it to spend time (however briefly) in a major entertainment or media monolith like Sony, MTV, CAA, HBO, and CBS. Not only because of the education and perspective you'll acquire—but the enormous number of potential contacts you'll meet. These people can be incredibly helpful for the entirety of your career. **Quality contact accumulation is the name of the game.**

There are two schools of thought operating here. Many people argue that taking a job in the business side of the entertainment, media or art worlds will educate you for the necessary selling, negotiating and promotion that is required by you to establish and maintain a creative livelihood. That it will galvanize you to understand the business of show. That it will allow you to understand how your agents and managers, producers, gallery owners and other buyers or gatekeepers operate. You will learn how, when and why they hire creatives. When you have your own reps, you will be in a better position to gauge their performance or lack thereof. You will also learn about the standard contracts, how to protect yourself and how much various creative professionals should expect to get paid.

Even better, you will be more prepared to make things happen for yourself without solely relying on reps, gatekeepers and others. This is one of the most important goals of this book. An additional advantage: you will have a much better idea how to sell yourself and your projects to these career success catalysts when you do interact with them. You will be much more knowledgeable about them, their careers and goals than if you are outside trying to figure out how to get noticed.

So, it's a no-brainer, right? Not exactly. Actually, the choice for a creative to work on the business side of his or her craft may have a number of cons depending on your business interest and abilities. **If you have a business interest and acumen, this is indeed be a no-brainer. I would strongly recommend it.**

You know who you are. If the prospect of having to work in a corporate environment is alienating if not horrifying: if the prospect of serving executives or creative icons makes you nauseous; if the prospect of no longer having a weekday free is claustrophobic; if the prospect of not being your own boss frustrates you bigtime, then you should immediately jump back to my **Survival Jobs Chapter.**

Something else to contemplate--what if you actually succeed, God forbid, on the business side? There are worse setbacks in life, but this would definitely sidetrack you from pursuing a purely creative path. Lack of time and energy may derail any creativity at all on your part. Even if you want to pursue your creative dreams, once you're accustomed to making serious bucks, it will be difficult, if not impossible, to start at the bottom financial rung again.

This is what essentially happened to me. I thought I would be at ICM for a year or two—that it was just a way station until I succeeded at being an actor or stand up comic or writer. To my great surprise, I was making much more significant progress (than my various creative careers) as an Agent. Because I am creative as well, I got along great with my clients—and loved to converse and joke with them. With actors, I would compete with them in doing accents or impressions. I made more cracks to my comedian clients than they made to me. I remember speaking in-depth with my journalist and news casting clients about those international political stories that never make it to the front pages. Most importantly, I never bullshitted my clients about anything—which they found enormously refreshing.

In terms of my creative pursuits, one of my problems is that I had too many disparate goals. Once again, **it is so essential to fulfill the requirements of a Primary Goal before trying to accommodate Secondary or other goals.** Another problem was I was generally too fatigued to spend much time in acting or stand-up classes, workshops and auditions. In other words, **a job on the business side of creative makes almost precludes you from strongly pursuing the creative side of the business.** This is particularly pronounced if you are pursuing work as a performer. I think it is much more doable as a writer, photographer or artist which can be pursued more easily during your leisure time. Of course, this is very influenced by your self-discipline and ability to manage your time.

Depending on your level of creative business success, you may also be pigeonholed (severely categorized) by the industry as a "suit" on the business side of entertainment, media or arts. This division is not easy to hurdle, believe you me. Once you gain a reputation on the business side of your craft, it will very hard to shake it off and go strictly creative. Or to earn respect as a creative. You can certainly try, but your business peers may never buy that you are a worthy creative professional. How could you be? How can you be so skilled at the business side and be a talented creative as well? It is entirely possible to be proficient in both business and creative sides, but many are too envious, skeptical or ignorant to believe this. **Don't ever let these naysayers influence or determine your own unique path.**

I know a number of producers, screenwriters and actors who actually use creative pseudonyms to overcome this horrible prejudice. They continue in their business roles and their colleagues/peers have no idea they are pursuing their creative dreams. Others will tell a small circle of confidantes. Whichever tactics serves your continuing creativity is the answer, my friends.

Without further ado, here is a dozen, in no particular order, of the most practical business jobs for creatives who don't mind starting on the ground floor:

1. Agent or Manager. Agencies and Management Companies can be a wealth of information. You will learn about contracts, standard terms and conditions, sales, negotiation and publicity. If you're working for someone brilliant, you may also absorb that rare, often elusive quality: taste. Beware of long hours, low pay and occasionally very abusive bosses.

2. Commercial or Industrial Production Company. Both provide skills and expertise that could lead to a lucrative career. However, if your sole dream is to make fictional films or television, you will be very frustrated and possibly offend the powers-that-be. If you're corporate or brand literate, this could be the place of your dreams.

3. Entertainment or Media Periodical/ Trade. Will become a maven about the news of your craft almost overnight. Definitely will know all cutting-edge industry news before anyone else. You can meet almost anyone you want to, particularly if you write well—and you have no real business being there if you don't. Your writing will improve dramatically, but the pay is nothing to write home about.

4. Entertainment Publicist. Extraordinary sales, marketing and telephone experience. Amazing contact accumulation with all media journalists, broadcasters and bloggers. Opportunity to bond and befriend the rich and famous—often, they trust you more than anyone else. Limitations on transferring to another creative business.

5. Film or Theater Investor. Next to impossible position to get unless you're related to them. You can meet whomever you want whenever you want. Everyone will want to know you. Small office and good hours. Investor may be indecisive or reluctant to ultimately invest. Be careful what you suggest to boss as it may be your last suggestion.

6. Film Sales Agent or Distributor. One month of this will make you forget two years of film school. Will gain a great perspective on the worldwide film industry. Tremendous comprehension of the word "commercial." Will learn sales, advertising, marketing and publicity and how these overlap. You better like producers, directors and watching countless films. Not wonderful salaries unless you own the company.

7. Government Funding Agency/Foundation/Grant Funding Organization. Difficult job to obtain—nepotism and cronyism is rampant. Very chilled work environment and intelligent, caring co-workers, although it can get political. Decent work hours. Every creative professional you know will want to intensify their friendship with you—like you just won the lottery. Almost no career advancement potential because few superiors want to leave.

8. Independent TV or Film Production Company. Decreasing supply of these jobs. Amazing opportunity to learn a variety of tasks and positions because their overhead is not large enough to hire specialists. Will meet an enormous number of contacts in your industry, particularly when your bosses cannot attend functions. You will learn to produce bigtime. Great talent interaction. They may work you much harder than you expected.

9. Personal Assistant to Actor, Director or Producer. If interacting with dozens of people on a daily basis is not your thing, this is a job that is usually conducted in a home, home-office, mansion-office, or small office. You can learn a lot quickly in this kind of job as you will do a lot more specialized tasks than you would in a large company. Will involve long hours. Contact accumulation with primary contacts is another strong point, although many will ignore you when you try to contact them after you leave.

10. Studio or Network. Don't despair if you're not in the ideal department or division. Once you prove yourself, you can always transfer. Can leapfrog upward, particularly if you bond with the right person. Premier meeting ground for future contacts. Executives can be very mean and dismissive. Great place to find a mentor and to clarify exactly what is right for you.

11. Theater or Art Gallery. Depending on your interests, these can be kinder, gentler places to work than larger companies. Much less of a division of labor equals more knowledge of the whole picture— and definite interaction with successful creatives. Great place to meet potential investors and philanthropists. May be too specialized. Usually very controlling bosses and limited advancement potential.

12. Topnotch Film Festival. Almost unparalleled opportunity to accumulate international film contacts quickly. Obviously, you must be crazy about films and those who make them. Mandatory to learn how to make top stars, directors and producers happy and comfortable, which may be much more difficult than you imagine. Endless hours (think retail), and, in the two months prior to the actual festival, no personal life whatsoever. Zippo.

If you are in doubt about whether you can handle a job in the business side of the entertainment, media or art industry, don't be afraid to get your feet wet. Get a job for six months to a year and then simply reassess. You will then be much more knowledgeable and have an undistorted and insider perspective about whether to stay or go. If you can stand it, I suggest planting your feet wherever you can continue to accumulate the largest flow of quality contacts—and keep on learning.

* * *

NEW OPPORTUNITIES IN NEW MEDIA

With fewer film distribution companies buying films, consolidating publishers buying fewer books, and many newspapers and magazines just trying to survive, you might be tempted to dwell in self-pity and look at the glass as half-empty. Don't you dare!

I'm an eternal optimist and I'd like to think that these times offer unparalleled opportunity for creativity. And unbelievable artistic control. Fewer MBA's, reps and gatekeepers pretending to have taste when they don't have a clue. Fewer middlemen and intermediaries who are geared to eliminate, discourage and steal much of your profits. **Never before has it been so inexpensive to create, shoot, produce and edit. The opportunity to make your creative mark has never been easier. So make something happen now!**

While you are waiting for a major accomplishment like a feature film or TV series to be to be made, it is also an incredibly effective way to **practice your craft**. That's right, to hone your skills and talents. Instead of freezing yourself and your abilities, instead of dreaming about the big break or the next big thing, this is an insanely rewarding way to expand, strengthen and stretch your creative muscles. It is also useful in finding both creative and business collaborators. You never really know people or how you gel with others until you work with them—until you see them under pressure. Indeed, you could find your artistic soul mate, the creative partner of a lifetime.

As writers, directors, actors, producers, artists and musicians, the Web can be a breeding ground for your creative exploration, discovery and knowledge. **If you don't happen to be a major name or icon, one of the most frustrating aspects of being a creative professional is the waiting. When is my next job coming? When**

will I be discovered? How will I be able to further my craft? When will my work be recognized?

Like you, I don't know the answers to these questions, but I do know that the Web/New Media has given you an amazing opportunity that you must embrace at once. No longer do you have the excuse to do very little. No longer do you have to wait or depend on your reps and gatekeepers alone for the next creative opportunity. Now you can make new art easily—there is every reason to give it a shot.

The promise of the Web/New Media is not just for aspiring creative professionals or young people, for that matter. One of the biggest mistakes made by working or even successful (which I define as ranging from paying your bills to being well-known) creative professionals is to ignore these new technological options. Try to take advantage of them as soon as you can. It is creative freedom at its best. No strict deadlines, creative pigeonholing or lack of creative control.

If you have any breathing space in your schedule, by all means collaborate with a friend or two that you haven't been able to, try a new genre, medium or duration; wear a new title or occupational hat, spread your wings and experiment in a way you never could when big money is at stake.

New Media (aka Alternative Television aka Webseries) is exploding in popularity. The best New Media webseries and personalities are now being highlighted in the traditional media. The big three social media sites: Facebook, LinkedIn and Twitter are all almost immediate delivery routes for the best of New Media. An important goal is for you and your work to have a strong presence on these sites. You should also consider: Google +, Reddit, Digg, Instagram, Pinterest, Tumblr, Stumbled Upon and Delicious. These social media engines can create, build and alert your own audience. In the process, you enhance your core brand: yourself.

A growing percentage of the Crowdfunding sites like TubeStart, Kickstarter, IndieGoGo and GoFundMe are successfully funding New Media projects. More than ever before, the majority of the public simply wants to see the final work and it doesn't mind if it comes via the Web. They may even prefer it. Even the big Hollywood agencies are in on the act—CAA, WME, ICM and UTA all have dedicated digital departments hungry to discover new content and highly skilled writer-directors.

It's never been easier to get your work out there. You can now distribute your film shorts on YouTube or Vimeo, blog to your heart's content, and let the public decide if they like your art without ever stepping foot in a gallery. Once again, **a very high percentage of those under 30 (e.g. millennials) are watching films or TV directly from computers, tablets and smart phones without relying on cable systems.** New Media is still, evolving but make no mistake, **there is a silent gold rush happening.** It is time for you to stake your claim!

A number of feature films that did not receive adequate distribution have been cut into bite-sized webseries and have received a lot more viewers than these projects would have attracted had they obtained basic independent distribution.

To promote your work effectively, always try to inform your potential audiences months in advance if possible. Let them know that your next project will soon be ready to be seen. Create a Facebook page and other home pages with any inviting information about your projects such as a teaser or trailer, brief summary or logline, photos, bios of principals involved and, if appropriate a director's or writer's statement.

Like the entertainment industry itself at present, New Media is in a state of flux. Despite the growth in choice, distribution outlets and popularity, there is not one set or formulaic way to earn money from the Web. Monetizing your work is no easy feat. Generally, it involves building an audience, communicating with them often and drawing them to support or finance your work.

Here are eight major avenues to earning money through New Media:

1. The YouTube Explosion: In the years since being bought by Google for $1.65 Billion in 2010, YouTube has funded over 160 partnerships with content providers for YouTube channels with over $350 million in investment. YouTube has disbursed big money to create hundreds of channels to be supplied by content providers or Multi-Channel Networks (MCN's). This money hasn't really trickled down to most independent content creators (particularly if you do not have a huge following), but hopefully this will change in the coming years. However, YouTube has created special partnerships with the most watched shows creating hundreds of content providers with earnings of over $100,000 per year. Some are New Media millionaires. The overwhelming majority of these successes are in the non-fiction arena. That is, they are critics or simply pontificate or goof about the subjects of their desire.

Check out such YouTube successes as: Rooster Teeth, Nostalgia Critic, freddiew, Hannah Hart, Annoying Orange, iJustine and Smosh to get a feel for what is working and why.

2. Advertising via CPM: CPM (Cost Per Thousand) advertising revenues through YouTube (e.g. Adsense), Hulu, Blip.TV, Web Series Channel, Koldcast.TV, Sci Final and a number of other websites are now offering their "content partners" some remuneration (the range is between $0.30-$2.50 CPM) for allowing advertising on your videos or blogs. The revenue distribution still needs to be adjusted in the favor of content providers. At present, the actual split with a MCN (e.g. YouTube takes 45%, the MCN 20%) leaves you with 35 percent. To offset this, many creators are monetizing their audience in a myriad of other ways including merchandising (see below) or directing their fans to their own website/blog where they have a degree of control. If you want to check who's making what on YouTube, www.socialblade.com is a great tool.

3. MCN's. Anyone in good standing can become a YouTube partner as long as you allow them to place advertising in, on and around your content, but it may be in your interest to partner with an MCN which can attract a larger audience, help support your content and make your channels easier to monetize. MCN's can also help creators in a variety of other ways: programming, collaboration, copyright management, and publicity. They can often provide better earnings through packaging, direct ad sales and sponsorship (see below). However, MCN's are not for everyone. Be aware that some of the big MCN's like Maker Studios and Machinima have been criticized (if not sued) by popular content providers who felt they were being shafted.

4. Merchandise: There are number of ways to earn money by selling merchandise to your following, whether it is T-shirts, stickers, hats, coffee mugs, extended DVD's or streams, or souvenirs from the show itself. Those who have popular blogs can obtain revenues through selling traditional or e-books.

5. Sponsorship: Many content providers, particularly those who appeal to a specific demographic, can sign sponsorship deals with suitable companies or brands to sell their product or create their own distinctive product to sell together. Sponsorship can also come in the form of financing (make sure to include salary in the front end because there probably will not be a backend) by a corporation (e.g. Ileana Douglass' IKEA-set and sponsored Webseries, "Easy to Assemble" which recently ended after four seasons), charity, political party or PAC (Political Action Committee), religion or a variety of non-profits.

If there is a substantial following, there is also the growing practice of direct ad sales between your content site and the advertising entity instead of through YouTube or other video distribution websites.

6. Licensing/Syndication: If you have a good relationship with a company, they may be willing to pay you to syndicate or redirect your work to their website. Make sure to read the contracts carefully so you don't dilute your brand or display your content on too many websites at once. The danger here is not getting the appropriate credit. Also, you don't want to compete with yourself in search engine ratings.

7. Subscription: Actually charging viewers for hard-earned (time and money) content. What a concept! If you have a YouTube channel and more than 10,000 followers, you are permitted to implement a subscription service. If you happen to have content that has a build-in audience or demand, you may find it profitable to reap the benefits of a subscription model. It is instructive to provide a trailer or teaser, and several free weeks so potential customers can have an initial taste. It also may be advisable to try this model on a trial basis. If it doesn't work, you can always go back to providing the content for free and use one of the other approaches described here.

8. Production/Publishing Deals: One potential benefit of having a popular fictional webseries or blog is to obtain a film, TV or publishing deal. This happened to a number of fictional webseries and blogs including "It's Always Sunny in Philadelphia" which was recently renewed for a tenth season on FX and "Shit My Day Says," which enjoyed a couple of seasons on CBS. There are several other webseries that have recently contracted with TV networks. There is also the opportunity to get traditional or e-book publishing deals for blogs or Twitter feeds. Do these deals happen often? No, but there is always the possibility if your content catches on. Exposure and expansion of your brand is also a great byproduct.

Those of you who want to monetize your blogs may also want to explore: Amazon Kindle's new blog publishing platform, NimbleNetwork, and Virurl, which also allows you to make money from your content.

The opportunities that are presented by the Internet are multiplying rapidly. Each week, more and more creatives are benefiting if not supporting themselves entirely from Web-based income. Just like social media networking, you cannot afford to ignore the business connection between the Web and your craft. However, that doesn't mean you can rely on it or quit your day job just yet. **Make an Olympian research effort and discover which websites and web distribution choices are right for you. Jump in as soon as you can.**

* * *

FAVORITE BOOKS AND WEBSITES

As you know by now, it's really important to continually improve your craft and sharpen your understanding of the business of your craft. I have provided my **Favorite Books and Websites** for this express purpose. However, I really don't want to go overboard with an endless list of my favorite sources because I don't want it to interfere with the time required for you to create and market your projects. Too many creative professionals use these sources as an excuse to avoid making things happen. They use it to procrastinate if not avoid doing their work altogether. These sources should be considered a bonus to be enjoyed like a dessert after a hard day's work.

BOOKS

ACTING
ACTING IN FILM *by Michael Caine*
ACTING PROFESSIONALLY *by Robert Cohen and James Calleri*
AUDITION *by Michael Shurtleff*
RESPECT FOR ACTING *by Uta Hagen*

ART
I'D RATHER BE IN THE STUDIO: The Artist's No-Excuse Guide to Self-Promotion *by Alyson B. Stanfield*

CREATING YOUR BRAND
BUILDING AN AUDIENCE: Fans, Friends and Followers *by Scott Kirsner*

CREATIVE SUCCESS
THE WAR OF ART *by Steven Pressfield*

CREATIVITY
STEAL LIKE AN ARTIST *by Austin Kleon*
THE ARTIST'S WAY *by Julia Cameron*

DIRECTING
ON DIRECTING *by Harold Clurman*
ON FILM-MAKING *by Alexander Mackendrick*

FILM MARKETING
SELLING YOUR FILM WITHOUT SELLING YOUR SOUL
by The Film Collaborative

SCREENWRITING
CREATING UNFORGETTABLE CHARACTERS *by Linda Seger*
MAKING A GOOD SCRIPT GREAT *by Linda Seger*
SAVE THE CAT *by Blake Snyder*
SCREENPLAY *by Syd Field*
SCREENWRITING FROM THE SOUL *by Richard W. Krevolin*
STORY *by Robert McKee*
TALK THE TALK: A Dialogue Workshop for Screenwriters *by Penny Penniston*
THE WRITERS JOURNEY *by Christopher Vogler*

STORY CREATION
STORYLINE: Finding Gold In Your Life Story *by Jen Grisanti*
THE HERO WITH A THOUSAND FACES *by Joseph Campbell*

WRITING
BECOMING A WRITER *by Dorothea Brande*
ON WRITING *by Stephen King*
WRITING DOWN THE BONES: Freeing the Writer Within *by Natalie Goldberg*

WEBSITES

ART
www.artbusiness.com
www.finearttips.com
www.theabundantartist.com

ENTERTAINMENT TRADES
www.hollywoodreporter.com
www.screendaily.com
www.variety.com

ENTERTAINMENT NEWS
www.deadlinehollywood.com
www.imdb.com
www.thewrap.com

INDEPENDENT FILM
www.filmmaker.com
www.filmmakermagazine.com
www.hopeforfilm.com
www.indiewire.com
www.withoutabox.com

MUSIC DISTRIBUTION
www.cdbaby.com
www.songcastmusic.com
www.tunecore.com

MUSIC BUSINESS
www.billboard.com
www.hypebot.com
www.musicindustryhowto.com

NEW MEDIA/SOCIAL MEDIA
www.forbes.com
www.reelseo.com
www.socialmediatoday.com

SCREENWRITING ART AND BUSINESS
www.dougrichardson.com
www.finaldraft.com
www.johnaugust.com
www.moviebytes.com
www.screenwritingutopia.com
www.scriptmag.com
www.trackingb.com (subscription)
www.wordplayer.com
www.writersstore.com

TECH
www.gigaom.com
www.mashable.com
www.techcrunch.com
www.wired.com

WRITING
www.dailywritingtips.com
www.quickanddirtytips.com/grammar-girl

NEVER STOP DOING IT!

Several years ago I found myself at the Edinburgh International Film & Theater Festival where I was presenting the play I produced, "Two Men Talking" as well as appearing on several film panels. I also used the opportunity to check out a few films including that of my friend, the gifted Slovenian director, Igor Sterk. After the screening of Igor's film, "Tuning," the Q & A session began in earnest when a robust and graying man raised his hand and complimented the film intelligently. I had seen and greeted this man at a number of other screenings throughout the festival. He was literally watching 5-7 films each day for an entire week!

The man then asked a series of precise and thoughtful questions which Igor answered superbly. When the Q & A session ended, I grabbed Igor to introduce him to this very engaging man. Igor was very surprised to realize it was the great Brian DePalma, the legendary, award-winning director of "Scarface," "The Untouchables" and "Carrie," to name a few.

We had a great conversation and then Mr. DePalma dragged us (in our jeans) to a black-tie party for all the stars, politicians and philanthropists behind the festival, but that's another story. The point is DePalma didn't have to watch 40 or 45 (primarily obscure foreign) films the week he was visiting this festival. He could have easily stayed in his hotel suite and socialized with movie stars and other renowned directors for all his stay. But he chose to educate himself by watching and studying all these films. Why did he do this?

Despite his massive creative achievements, Brian DePalma did not rest on his laurels alone. He was still hungry to improve himself creatively. To Keep on Learning. To appreciate the cutting edge international filmmaking that year. To stretch and expand himself creatively. To acquaint himself with the latest in excellent writing, directing and cinematography around the globe.

Most of the great or legendary creative professionals never stop improving and honing their craft. To this day, Al Pacino, Robert De Niro, and Nicole Kidman still refresh themselves between films with acting classes or private coaching sessions. Numerous successful film directors work on shorter projects to practice or stretch—that is, try a different genre or medium for example. Renowned musicians go to the country or urban studios simply to learn from and jam with their peers. Novelists, journalists and artists will go to various retreats around the world to work on their craft and learn from others in their field.

Never stop improving. Whatever your artistic achievements, you must resist the temptation to cocoon, to become too attached to your hometown or city (even if it's LA or NY), or to be competitive with your peers. You need to reach out and interact with them now and then. As an artist, you are duty-bound to constantly improve your craft. You must always be on lookout for ways to expand yourself and your craft. You should ask yourself: What can I do to improve? Who can help me do so? What are my creative weaknesses? Are my talents competitive and up-to-date with those who are making a living in my chosen field? If not, what is missing? Are there any adjustments I can make?

Then it is up to you to do the research and interviews to find the right teachers, seminars, workshops, conferences, coaches, retreats, festivals to help you get where you need to be creatively.

The best artists and creatives are those who are flexible enough to change course or revise, revise, revise—whether it is their strategy, career goals or specialties. The best artists and creatives are also willing to be self-critical and improve themselves. Not too self-critical, mind you, but enough to continually guide themselves to creative career success. Are there any (preferably more established) friends or peers you can ask to evaluate your work? Try to avoid being overly sensitive or defensive in this regard. You don't have to take any or all of their advice, but it's a good reality check to hear what others think of the current state of your craft.

Never stop stretching. Yes, you have read this elsewhere is this text, but besides practicing and honing your craft it is incumbent upon you to creatively stretch yourself as much as you can. Take risks and try something different. It may be a more demanding medium, genre, duration or role. However glowing the reviews and feedback you may receive, you should still make an effort to stretch yourself. This will be beneficial in ways you can't even imagine. Who knows? Maybe you're still not aware of where your greatest talent really lies. Stretching can lead you to further success and quite possibly, a new and more interesting creative direction for your career. More importantly, it makes your craft (not to mention, creativity) more interesting, alive and fresh.

Never stop learning. One of the major goals of this book is for you to understand the business side of your craft and make a living or better living from it. But are you reading and watching all you can about your craft? **At present, there are an enormous variety of resources out there for you to re-energize your craft, from books to magazines, web articles to websites, videos, seminars, workshops, conferences, panels and classes of all types. Learn from your creative peers and study with the best teachers in the world. Some resources will be of limited use, but others will be absolutely essential to exercising, maintaining and transforming your craft into the future. Once you succeed, I'll be your biggest fan!**

* * * * * * *

ACKNOWLEDGEMENTS

I would like to thank the exceptional Colleen Bent for her love, support, technical know-how, kindness and generosity. Not to mention her calmness during my technical temper tantrums.

I am so grateful to my brilliant and loving brother Steve Jermanok, who is one of the world's most prolific travel writers and bloggers, having explored more than 90 countries and written over 1500 articles on a broad range of subjects, from food to art to adventure. His support has been unyielding. He is also a consummate editor who invested a lot of time and energy into making this book professional and clean, very clean. And essentially stopped me from starting sentences with "And"... for the most part anyway.

Many, many thanks to Steve's truly amazing wife, Lisa Leavitt, for her enthusiasm and permission to occupy their home in suburban Boston to finish this book. They also run an amazingly popular boutique travel agency, *www.activetravels.com.*

I doubt I would have successfully released this book without the guidance and expertise of the incomparable book designer Rosen Dukov, who is also one of the most respected digital designers and artists in Europe—not to mention a very gifted visual visionary and entrepreneur. I am so fortunate to have him as my partner in our new global webseries LIFEADVICE.TV or *www.lifeadvice.tv.* It is a dynamic and revolutionary webseries that gives our wisest people a voice and the rest of us some guidance in our lives.

I also want to express my appreciation to the literary agent and publisher Lisa Hagan who tried to make this book a reality.

Before this became a book, I did hundreds of workshops world-wide on the same subject and want to thank my local promoters and gifted creative professionals: Jennifer Gjulameti, Erica Derrickson, Jenna Sullivan, Mike Messier, and Danielle Thys.

I appreciate the wise advice from entertainment executive and author, Adam Leipzig, who urged me to get this book out there at once.

I am so so grateful to my hardworking and exceptional interns/assistants whom I am certain will be all be ridiculously successful: Natalia Dasilva, Ariana Lambdin, Alia Azamat and Mary Vade Bon Coeur.

My extremely generous and loving sister Fawn Schechter and her witty husband Jack Schechter who have always been there for me.

Last but not least, my love to my four insanely gifted and accomplished nieces and nephews: Sarah Schechter, Jake Jermanok, Max Schechter and Melanie Jermanok. I know these four college students will enjoy reading this and may even try to convince their creative classmates to do the same.

ABOUT THE AUTHOR

Jim Jermanok is an award-winning writer, director and producer in film, TV and New Media; creative entrepreneurship expert, consultant and speaker. His words and photos can be seen in *The Washington Post*, *Indiewire*, *The Huffington Post* and *The Boston Globe*.

He wrote and produced the highly acclaimed romantic comedy, "Passionada," which was released by Columbia Tri Star in over 150 countries. His film "Em" won the Grand Jury Prize at the Seattle International Film Festival, and Best Producer Award at the Brooklyn Intl. Film Festival, among other honors. Most recently, Jim wrote and directed "Homophonia," a political comedy about gay marriage rights that has appeared at over 50 film festivals while winning several.

His revolutionary new web series "LIFEADVICE.TV" has drawn high praise since going live globally in 2015. Mr. Jermanok is a former ICM Entertainment Agent who helped to represent Arthur Miller, Shirley MacLaine, Ben Kingsley, Dudley Moore, Helen Hayes, Alan Arkin and General H. Norman Schwarzkopf, among others. For writing, consulting and speaking/workshop services, please contact him at: getreelgetreel@gmail.com or www.jimjermanok.com.

Jim Jermanok
BEYOND THE CRAFT:
What You Need to Know to MakeA Living Creatively!

American, First Edition

Web: www.jimjermanok.com
Facebook: jermanok
LinkedIn: jimjermanok
Twitter: getreelgetreel

ISBN: 978-0-692-77576-9

Made in the USA
Columbia, SC
06 January 2019